10

BRIAN BORU
& THE BATTLE FOR IRELAND

14

Morgan Llywelyn

Since 1978 Morgan Llywelyn, who lives north of Dublin, has published nineteen historical novels about Ireland and the Celtic peoples, including such international bestsellers as *Lion of Ireland*, *Red Branch*, *Druids*, and the five volumes of her critically acclaimed *Irish Century* series. Her published work also includes a non-fiction biography of Xerxes of Persia, a number of short stories and eight books for younger readers. She received the Best Novel of the Year Award from Penwoman International, the Poetry and Prose Award from the Galician Society, the Book of the Year from the American Libraries Association, the Saint Brendan Medal from the Brendan Society, two Bisto Awards and the biannual Readers' Association of Ireland Award. She was named Exceptional Celtic Woman of the Year by Celtic Women International; nominated by the Irish Writers' Union for the Nobel Prize for Literature 1996; was a judge for the Fish Short Story Prize 2001, and a judge for the Dublin IMPAC International Literary Award 2003; nominated for the IMPAC Award 2007; named to 100 Top Irish Americans, *Irish American Magazine* 2008; and received the Irish Books and Media Award for Outstanding Contribution to Literature in 2012. An early member of the Irish Writers' Centre, Llywelyn has served as chairman of the Irish Writers' Union and as a trustee of the Irish Children's Book Trust. She also undertook long-distance walks to raise money for various charities, and in 1998 walked from Clare to Clontarf, the journey of Brian Boru.

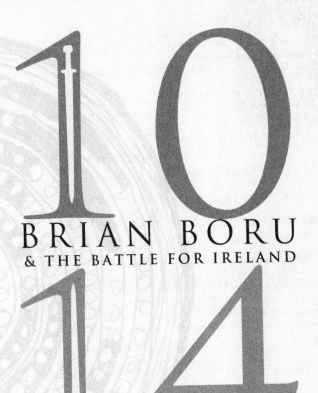

1014

BRIAN BORU
& THE BATTLE FOR IRELAND

MORGAN LLYWELYN

THE O'BRIEN PRESS
DUBLIN

First published 2014 by The O'Brien Press Ltd.
12 Terenure Road East, Rathgar,
Dublin 6, Ireland.

Tel: +353 1 4923333; Fax: +353 1 4922777
E-mail: books@obrien.ie.
Website: www.obrien.ie

ISBN: 978-1-84717-557-1

Illustrations by Emma Byrne
Map artwork by Anú Design (www.anu-design.ie)

1 2 3 4 5 6 7 8 9 10
14 15 16 17 18 19 20

Printed in Denmark by Nørhaven
The paper in this book is produced using pulp from managed forests

Dedication:

For Patricia MacMahon and, as always, for Charlie

CONTENTS

AUTHOR'S NOTE

Most of the Irish names in this book are given a pronounceable English equivalent. For example, Briain Bórumha becomes Brian Boru; Maelseachlainn Mór becomes Malachy Mór, and Dubhchobhlaigh is rendered as Duvcholly. Gormlaith (Gormfhlaith in Irish) is an exception, due to her notoriety. Her name is pronounced Gurmla, but she is far better known as Gormlaith. Place-names also are given in English. Dates conform to the Christian calendar as it was used in Ireland in 1014 of the Current Era.

Foreword by
The O'Brien, Prince of
Thomond
18ᵗʰ Baron Inchiquin

Morgan Llywelyn, one of the world's most successful and respected historical novelists writing about Ireland and the Celtic culture, has departed from fiction to present a factual history of one of Ireland's milestone events.

1014: The Battle of Clontarf, is one of the first dates that an Irish child learns in school. 1014 is as significant for Ireland as 1066 and the Battle of Hastings were for the English. In this groundbreaking book published in 2014, its millennium year, Llywelyn employs her unique skills to bring the Battle of Clontarf to life once more. She offers not just a recitation of the names and dates but a vivid glimpse into the past in all its dramatic and bloody reality. She has an uncanny knack of carrying the reader back through time and a deep, almost intuitive understanding of ancient Ireland.

Llywelyn's approach to the Battle of Clontarf takes a fresh look at the generally accepted accounts which have been written and re-written over the centuries. Scholars and historians continue to argue over who was there and what happened that day. Llywelyn is not afraid to widen the posts of historical interpretation and possibilities. Nor is she reluctant to seek out the answers others have overlooked. The result is an historical account to stand with Cecil Woodham-Smith's *The Reason Why* about the Charge of the Light Brigade.

The author's intensive study of Brian Boru began with research for her international bestseller *Lion of Ireland*, and has continued ever since, focusing on the character of Ireland's greatest high king as demonstrated through his actions. Drawing upon her unique understanding of Brian, now Llywelyn has produced an authentic portrait of the man who worked so hard to assure Ireland of lasting peace and prosperity – until the triumph and tragedy of 1014.

As a direct descendant of Brian Boru and Chief of the Name, I believe we O'Briens are lucky indeed to have Morgan Llywelyn as our modern day bard.

The Rt. Hon. Conor O'Brien, the Lord Inchiquin

INTRODUCTION

B rian Boru is a prominent figure in the histories
of early medieval Ireland, yet when my historical
novel, *Lion of Ireland*, was first published in 1980 there
was no other book in print about Ireland's most famous
high king. No biography of him existed. Some of the
people with whom I discussed the project in the beginning assured me that Brian was a fictional hero from
Celtic folklore, like Cúchulainn or Fionn mac Cumhaill.
There could have been no such person because Irish historical heroes were always failures. Everyone knew that,
they said. And even if someone of that name had existed,
nothing was known about him. They said.

They were wrong on both counts. Brian Boru was
a real person. Determined research uncovered enough
information to construct a novel around him, though I
did not stop there.

SOURCES

The known facts about Brian are contained within several Irish annals compiled contemporaneously with or

11

shortly after his life, as well as a few Norse texts. All of the subsequent accounts over the centuries have been taken from this material and reworked according to the opinions and prejudices of the writers and historians involved. These have provided an endless source of controversy and will continue to do so into the far future.

Since *Lion of Ireland* became an international bestseller, numerous writers and scholars as well as film makers have rediscovered Brian and wanted to retell his story. All face the same problem I did: when it comes to documentation there are only the archaic records to draw upon, and those can be contradictory and confusing. Beyond them everything is and must be speculation, conjecture, and educated guesswork.

My continuing interest in the character and career of Brian Boru has resulted in the collection of a sizeable library devoted to him and the world he inhabited (see the partial bibliography at the end of the book). In 1983 Roger Chatterton Newman published the first non-fiction biography of Brian, *Brian Boru, King of Ireland*. And 1990 saw the publication of my book for young readers entitled *Brian Boru, Emperor of the Irish*, which won the Bisto Award for Excellence. As we approach the thousandth anniversary of Brian's greatest battle, it seems appropriate to revisit Clontarf and make an effort to understand what really happened on Good Friday, 1014. The foreign invaders combined with the rebel Irish had superior numbers and weaponry, yet Brian Boru won. The great question is – how?

Writing an accessible non-fiction history of the Battle of Clontarf was a challenge. In 1986–87 I had published *Xerxes*, a biography of the Persian warrior-king commissioned by City College of New York, and was familiar with the task of reconstructing ancient battles. To set the events of 1014 in context required a condensed outline of the socio-political situation of Ireland in the late ninth century and a re-examination of the known facts.

But more was necessary to open up this story to a wider audience. Both historians and biographers employ speculation to address gaps left in the fabric of the distant past. As a historian I have great respect for the facts; as a novelist I appreciate the drama and sense of immediacy that fiction can produce. No fact or incident has been invented in this book, but if their history is to be more than dry bones the people involved needed to be given flesh and blood, and have some of the small details of their everyday lives brought to light. The techniques of a novelist have been employed to set scene and atmosphere. The best-known legends surrounding Brian and the battle have been included because they are such an integral part of the whole. Still, there is so much we cannot really know, including the motives and emotions of the men and women who lived a thousand years ago. These are the elements which allow the greatest latitude for conjecture; humans are always the most intriguing.

Three things are certain: Brian Boru actually lived. A great battle took place in 1014. And Ireland won.

★ ★ ★

I wish to thank Éamonn de Burca of de Burca's Rare Books for helping me on the initial, sometimes frustrating search for material about Brian Boru's Ireland. Without Éamonn's guidance I would never have located some of the more obscure works now in my personal collection. The late Cornelius Howard of the Department of Foreign Affairs introduced me to the owners of private libraries, here and abroad, who let me study rare manuscripts that were not available to the public. Professor George Meier, then head of the Department of Celtic Studies in Georgetown University, Washington, D.C. gave me access to important material which had long since left Ireland. The Rt. Hon. Conor O'Brien, the Lord Inchiquin, who is thirty-second in the line of descent from Brian Boru, graciously provided me with family details not available anywhere else.

Public libraries in both Dublin and County Clare have

been of help with this project, as have numerous conversations with military experts. The National Library of Ireland has been the principal source for maps relating to pre-Norman Ireland, while thanks go to the Dublin Civic Museum for providing topographical details, and to the Irish Meteorological Office for their tidal calculations.

Dublin and its environs have changed drastically since 1014. The blood-soaked battlefield where so many fought and died lies under tonnes of earth, obliterated by a thousand years of haphazard construction. In 1979 the extensive remains of Viking Dublin – the largest such settlement outside of Scandinavia, and a treasure trove of irreplaceable archaeology – were bulldozed and buried beneath new civic offices by Dublin Corporation.

A person visiting Clontarf today expecting to see the battlefield would be in for a shock. The topography of north Dublin has been totally reshaped. Therefore special thanks are due to the late historian Éamonn Mac Thomáis and to the intrepid Frank Cullen. Three decades apart, these two men generously accompanied me on foot-by-foot explorations of the area which was once a battleground, as proved by the many artefacts found there. The purpose was to correlate distances, elevations and viewing points with the annalists' descriptions of the events.

In 1988 broadcaster Donncha Ó Dulaing invited me to join in walking from Clare to Clontarf. Our party of dedicated walkers spent fourteen strenuous days following in the footsteps of Brian Boru on his way to the great battle, although our purpose was to raise money for charity rather than to fight invaders. No research book could equal the actual physical experience of the march, and I can never thank Donncha enough. Sincere thanks also to the scholars, historians and military enthusiasts, too numerous to name, who contributed in other ways to the compilation of this book. Each of you provided a piece of the puzzle. Any errors within these pages are entirely my own.

Lastly, but by no means least, I wish to thank Michael O'Brien and his talented team at The O'Brien Press for giving me this opportunity to revisit Brian and his Ireland one more time.

Morgan Llywelyn, Dublin, 2013

IRELAND
in 1014

aileach

River Finn   River Foyle   River Bann

River Derg   ULSTER   Lough Neagh

River Erne   River Blackwater   River Bann   River Logan

Lough Erne

Lough Conn   Lough Allen

River Moy   River Shannon   River Annalee   River Foyle   **Armagh**

Lough Gara   **Carlingford**

Lough Mask   connacht   Lough Sheelin   River Boyne

River Clare   Lough Kee   meath

Lough Corrib   River Suck   River Brosna   **Tara**

River Shannon   River Liffey   **Howth**

Dublin

leinster

kincora

River Shannon   River Nore   River Slaney

Limerick

Cashel   River Barrow

munster   River Suir   **Wexford**

River Laune   River Blackwater   **Waterford**

River Lee   **Cork**

desmond

n
w   e
s

Map artwork by Anú Design (www.anu-design.ie)

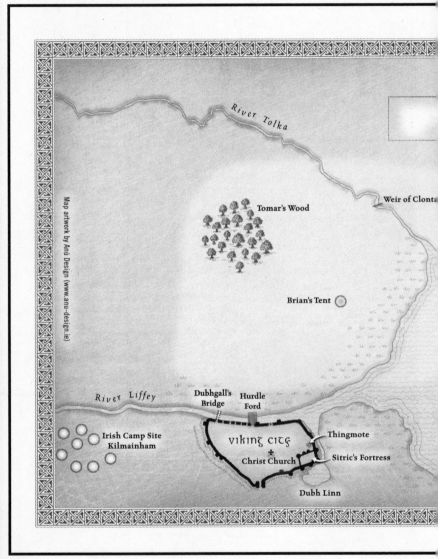

River Tolka

Weir of Clonta

Tomar's Wood

Brian's Tent

River Liffey

Dubhgall's Bridge

Hurdle Ford

Irish Camp Site Kilmainham

VIKING CITY

Christ Church

Thingmote

Sitric's Fortress

Dubh Linn

Map artwork by Anú Design (www.anu-design.ie)

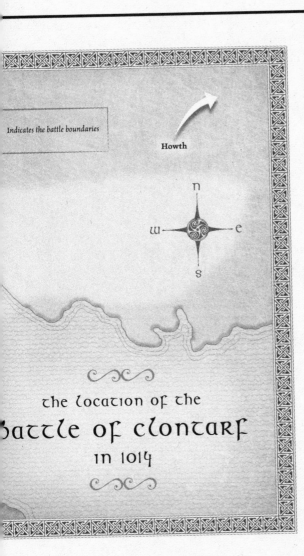

Indicates the battle boundaries

Howth

n
w e
s

the location of the
battle of clontarf
in 1014

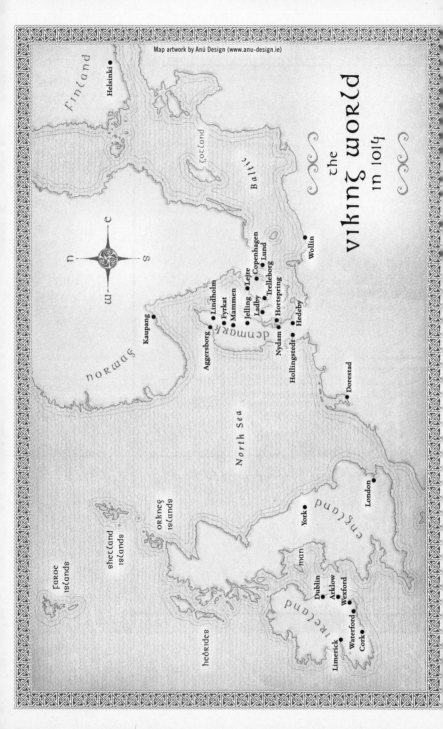

Map artwork by Anú Design (www.anu-design.ie)

the viking world
in 1014

finland

Helsinki

scotland

Baltic

Wollin

norway

Kaupang

denmark

Lindholm
Fyrkat
Mammen
Jelling
Ladby
Lejre
Copenhagen
Lund
Trelleborg
Hortspring
Aggersborg
Nydam
Hedeby
Hollingstedr
Dorestad

North Sea

faroe islands

shetland islands

orkney islands

hebrides

man

england

York

London

Ireland

Dublin
Arklow
Wexford
Limerick
Waterford
Cork

PROLOGUE: MORNING

Battle morning! A warrior spirit thrills to those words. This day might see the greatest battle of all, the one which a man will remember for the rest of his life. He can tell the story over and over again to his grandchildren and warm his cold bones by the fire of their admiration. He may even become a legend.

Battle morning!

Few had slept well the night before. Even the most experienced campaigners were restless, as men are restless when there is a storm gathering and the air is heavy with foreboding. New recruits had listened eagerly to the talk of the veterans, trying to grasp clues as to the future. But around the campfires the seasoned fighters had talked about the food or the weather or the long march they had just endured. Hardly any spoke of their women at home and none mentioned their children. The impending battle was not discussed by men who knew they had little control over its outcome. Awake before first light, they lay on their backs and stared at the sky, waiting for the stars to fade. Wondering who would be alive to observe the next appearance of the stars.

Advance scouts had been reporting to the command camp all night. The tall old man who had not slept listened to them with folded arms, assessing the information they brought. Sometimes he nodded. Sometimes he merely raised his head and turned a serious face towards the east, visualising. He carried it all in his head as he had carried everything in his head for so many years – the dreams, the plans, the strategies. All in one head, which was too valuable to risk in battle now, according to his sons.

His eyes burned with exhaustion. He passed one hand over them, a huge, still-powerful hand – had it not killed an opponent in single combat just the year before? He would defer to his sons' wishes because it was time to let the burden of responsibility pass to them, but he would keep his sword by his side.

Tomorrow, when the victory was won, he could sleep.

The April sky turned a translucent green with the coming of the dawn. The date was Good Friday, 23 April in the Year of Our Lord 1014. The most ferocious battle ever fought in Ireland was about to begin.

• • • • • • •

CHAPTER ONE

IRELAND

I n 1014 Ireland did not think of itself as a nation or as a political entity. The concept of 'nationhood' was unknown. Poets referred to the land of many tribes as Erin, after an ancient goddess named Eriu. The inhabitants called themselves the Gael, or the Scoti. On maps drawn by the geographers of antiquity the island west of Britain was called Hibernia, from the Latin word *hibernus*, meaning 'wintry'.

The Gael of Ireland belonged to one of several branches descended from a passionate and energetic warrior race whom the early Greeks identified as the Keltoi, or Celts. As with most things concerning the Celts, there is controversy about their origins, even about their right to be called a race. The Celtic homeland is described as extending from Bohemia in Germany to Silesia in southwestern Poland. The majority of modern anthropologists trace the Celts through their linguistic ties back to the Indo-Europeans, people of the steppes north of the Black Sea who migrated throughout continental Europe before the third millennium BC and became one of the foundations of western civilisation.

Archaeological studies indicate that the Gael reached Ireland by sea around the end of the Bronze Age. They brought iron weapons with them, enabling them to supplant the Bronze Age inhabitants who, in turn, had replaced Neolithic Man. At first the settlers probably intermarried with the surviving natives. There were no more incomers. For over a thousand years the Gael held undisputed sway over the land of Ireland. Great courage, a love of beauty, and a reverence for the natural world were amongst the qualities they admired and pursued. This was the culture that eventually produced the Book of Kells, the Tara Brooch, thousands of other works of art, and the Brehon law, which was described in 1987 by the Rt Honourable John J Flaherty, Chief Justice of Pennsylvania as 'the most humane and realistic legal system ever devised'. But more of that later.

From their point of view, the Gael had found paradise

at the edge of the Atlantic. Their island, which is about the size of the American state of Maine, was rich in the natural resources needed to support a pastoral, semi-nomadic lifestyle. The movement of glaciers during the Ice Age had carved the island into a fertile central plain ringed by coastal highlands. Although in the same latitude as Labrador, Ireland benefited from mild southwesterly winds and the warm waters of the Gulf Stream, which created a temperate climate. The island as a whole was a near-wilderness of timeless beauty. Much of the land was covered by expanses of mixed forest, primarily oak, but also hazel, ash, rowan, holly and yew. Thus there was an endless supply of timber to build shelter and to fuel fires. Field and forest abounded with game, rivers and lakes swarmed with fish, and the coasts provided a wide variety of shellfish. There also were deposits of gold, silver and copper to create the spectacular personal ornaments beloved of the Gael.

With everything they needed provided by the island on which they lived, the Gael had little inclination to venture further afield. A few did turn to piracy, harrying British sea lanes and occasionally seizing slaves; Saint Patrick was first brought to Ireland as a slave. For the most part, the Gael lived much as their warrior forebears had done on the European continent. Surrounded by water on all sides, Ireland was isolated for many centuries. The male population had no one to hone their battle skills upon but one another. This they did, with gusto. The tribes fought each other until battle became both sport and art, a way of life by which they defined themselves.

During the first millennium after Christ, Ireland contained between 100 and 150 semi-autonomous petty kingdoms, each made up of several tribes. Every tribe had its own chieftain; every kingdom had its own king who was elected from amongst the suitable members of the most powerful tribe. These petty kings had the right to demand tribute, a form of tax which usually consisted of cattle and warriors, from the tribes in their territory. They raised armies to fight other kings for territorial conquest, for the enforcement of hegemony, or to plunder and weaken a rival kingdom. The size and prosperity of the individual kingdoms waxed and waned with the fortunes of war. The victors were immortalised by the poets.

To add to the divisiveness, the island consisted of five separate and semi-autonomous provinces: Ulster (Uladh in Irish) in the north; Leinster (Laighin) in the east; Connacht (Connachta) in the west; Munster (Mumhan) in the south; and in the centre, Meath (Mídhe), the royal province. These were ruled by provincial kings to whom the petty kings in their territory owed tribute. The provincial kings, in turn, owed tribute to an overlord known as the Árd Rí, or high king, whose traditional seat was at Tara in Meath. Tara today is a long grassy ridge often occupied by grazing sheep. From its elevation on a clear day one can see mountains in each of the other four provinces, a kingly view indeed.

In no stage of Irish history had the term 'high king' implied monarchy. No high king governed all of Ireland. The Árd Rí reigned but did not rule. His subjects were the provincial kings who owed him tribute and courted his patronage to support their individual power. This arrangement likewise controlled the downward dispersion of property through petty kings and clan chieftains. Below the nobles were the freemen, and on the lowest rung of the ladder, the slaves, most of whom were captives taken in war. Slavery was not a permanent condition. A slave could buy his or her freedom, and many did.

The office of king, of whatever rank, was elective. In the case of the provincial kings and the high king it was restricted to the princely class, which included anyone whose great-grandfather had been a king. Male members of this class were obliged to undergo a very specific training, both mental and physical. The eldest son of a king did not automatically inherit his father's role. So long as there was an eligible member of his family who had the support of the other tribes, that person might accede to the kingship if he was of the age, strength, and character to suit the office. Thus the method of choosing a king was not fully one of merit, nor fully elective, nor fully hereditary, but a combination of all three. In the case of the Árd Rí, the family from which he came was of paramount importance. For centuries the high king was elected from either the northern or southern branches of the Uí Néill, the family with the longest history of high kingship.

Until one man changed that.

The Gael developed a highly stratified society conforming to an elaborate system known as Brehon law. Brehons were judges, members of the intellectual class that included teachers, healers, and bards. Bards were highly revered – a poet was considered the equal of a prince, a gifted satirist could topple a king. Brehons, as interpreters of the law, were concerned with every aspect of tribal life, from governing the election of kings to writing statutes concerning beekeeping.

Under Brehon law women had a degree of equality with men. Whether single or married they could inherit property and conduct its usage. The importance of women's work was shown by the value assigned to their implements: a needle used in embroidery was valued at an ounce of silver, or part ownership of a yearling heifer. In case of divorce, which was common in early Ireland, a woman's dowry might be returned to her. Polygamy was accepted if all parties consented, although in certain circumstances, such as incest, adultery was punishable by death. There was no such thing as illegitimacy: any act which resulted in a child was considered a marriage. There were no orphans. If a child's parents were dead, he or she was fostered by other members of the tribe.

Because the pre-Christian Gael had no written language, their history was painstakingly memorised by their bards over a period as long as twenty years. Poetry in its primitive form was a chant of pure emotion, speaking directly to the spirit. Captured in poetry like a fly in amber, Ireland's history and genealogies were transmitted from one generation to the next virtually intact.

In the sixth century, Christianity arrived in Ireland together with its concomitant literacy. The new faith was superimposed on the ancient druidic tradition without a substantial struggle. Ireland underwent an

almost bloodless conversion as kings and princes gradually accepted fresh ideas. The majority of the Gael, who
had a long history of loyalty to their chosen leaders,
followed them into the worship of Christ. Canon law
took its place beside Brehon law in Gaelic society. For
a long time observance appears to have been optional,
however.

The people remained pastoral. The only towns of
any size were those which developed around monastic centres. Tribal warfare continued unabated; cattle
raids were as frequent as ever. Bands of outlaws, even if
avowed Christians, were not above looting a monastery.

Literacy offered a fresh outlet for the artistic impulse.
Masterpieces like the Book of Kells testify to a new
faith and a soaring imagination. Christian craftsmen
turned native gold and silver into objects of breathtak-
ing beauty, such as the Ardagh Chalice. The Ireland of
saints and scholars existed for several generations – but
it could not last.

If the Gael were content to stay at home, others
were not. The last decade of the eighth century saw
the arrival of the Vikings. Their power in Ireland would
reach its zenith with the Battle of Clontarf.

'Viking' was an appellation applied impartially to sea
rovers from Norway and Denmark, as well as to adven-

turers from Sweden, Jutland, Iceland, and the islands and coasts of the Baltic. These people did not actually call themselves Vikings until the twelfth century, however. The origin of the word *viking* is something of a mystery. It may have been a verb describing what the Scandinavians did during three centuries of their history: they were seagoing marauders, they were Northmen who went 'viking'.

Another term applied to them was 'Land Leaper', meaning someone who seizes another's land. During the cold, dark, interminable nights of winter in northern Europe, a man could only dream of the sun − of green grass, of golden fields of grain. Dream ... and long ... and ultimately determine to find. And seize for himself. This very human urge motivated one of the most violent eras in history, but it was not the only cause.

A rise in the population of Scandinavia, which began in the seventh century, reached a climax in the tenth, putting great pressure on land and resources. Added to this was the resentment of the Norse *jarls*, or noblemen, with their own independent earldoms, at efforts being made to unify Norway under one crown.

The result of these forces coming together was an explosion of Vikings onto the world stage.

As with most of early history, facts about this period

have been exaggerated and embellished until the underlying kernel of truth may be hard to find. A predilection for embroidering history is not unique to the Irish. Down through the ages famous historians have refused to let the truth get in the way of a colourful story. Plato, Herodotus, Giraldus Cambrensis – and that master propagandist, Julius Caesar – all employed creative fiction to suit their purposes. Thus it is not surprising that something as momentous in its time as the Battle of Clontarf has been heavily mythologised. The protagonists were always prime candidates for myth – none more so than the Vikings.

During the ninth and tenth centuries the political situation in Ireland had changed dramatically. Adding Vikings to the mix destabilised a complex societal structure built on blood and hereditary ties, an archaic code of law, and shifting military alliances. It also seemed to herald an increase in violence among the native Irish, who could not fail to be affected by the actions of the invaders.

The Norse and Swedes, whom the Gael identified as 'the fair foreigners' in the beginning, and the Danes, whom they described as 'the dark foreigners', often fought among themselves – not unlike the Irish. The Viking concept of warfare was somewhat different, however. They considered battle an end in itself, a transforming experience which could open the gates to Valhalla, their idea of heaven. The Gael usually respected their dead enemies. The Vikings practised a variety of mutilations on theirs. Two of the most frequently cited examples are revealing. In one, a man was propped against a tree while still alive, eviscerated, then bound to the tree with his own intestines. The second example is the notorious and not infrequent 'blood eagle'. A man's lungs were torn from his living body and placed on his back, like wings. It is little wonder that the word 'viking' could instil terror.

Yet within a couple of generations many of the Vikings in Ireland had become settlers in the literal meaning of the word. They settled. And as emigrants tend to do, they clung to their own kind. They formed communities which grew into towns – a foreign concept in such a pastoral culture. Wicklow and Arklow in the southeast were two of their earliest successes.

As Norse and Dane adjusted to the more moderate climate of their new land they grew comfortable, even prosperous. Trading centres proliferated and eventually became the focal point of towns. Bunratty Castle in County Clare stands on what was the site of a Viking trading post in 970. In Ireland the growing season was longer and the soil was warmer, so farms were laid out in the hinterland of the towns. Families expanded in response to the change in circumstances. Immigrants married Irish women, or, rarely, brought women from their homeland, built houses and raised children. Memories of the cold north faded into tales told to the little ones around the fire. The newcomers ceased to be, if they ever had been, the rampaging Vikings of song and saga.

Ultimately the Norse became the predominant Scandinavian element in Ireland. After changing hands several times between Norse and Dane, Dublin became the nucleus of the smaller Danish population. However, the phrase 'The Danes of Dublin' entered into common usage to such an extent that eventually all Northmen were called Danes. This created a confusion which continues to influence historians today – although some go the other way, and call all the Danes 'Norsemen'.

Around the coasts of the island various Gaelic tribes developed trading relationships with the newcomers. One result was valuable cultural and linguistic cross-pollination, which engendered a growing if grudging respect. But tribes elsewhere in Ireland went to war against the foreigners, striving to expel or at least dominate them. War was too old a habit to relinquish in favour of trade. In a society where the greatest honours were achieved in battle, commerce was considered less than noble. *The Annals of the Four Masters,* which document early and medieval Irish history in great detail and was compiled in the seventeenth century, contain hundreds of accounts of great battles and heroic undertakings, but none of commercial success.

Many of the written records of the period were lost when Vikings – or raiding parties of Irish outlaws, who were just as bad – burned or stole countless books and manuscripts. There is no excuse for the Irish, but until they were Christianised the Vikings could not read, and so did not value what they had taken. They knew enough to sell them, though, or at least to steal the jewels with which many books and sacred objects were embellished. In this way a number of priceless artefacts found their way to the European continent. A few eventually came home again.

The surviving ancient Irish texts, fragmentary though they are, stand as documents of the era in which they were written. Thanks to the efforts of scholars and archaeologists many can now be dated with reasonable certainty. The identities of individuals as well as historical details have been verified. We know to a degree what happened at Clontarf on Good Friday, 1014. We can recognise the event for what it was: a Greek tragedy of classical proportions. Its central figure was a giant by any standards. He was known as Brian Boru.

• • • • • • •

CHAPTER TWO

Ireland in the Tenth Century

In AD 941 a son was born into a large clan in the kingdom of Thomond, a territory in the province of Munster. His parents had him christened Brian. Their clan, or group of closely related families, belonged to the tribe of the Dál gCais: the Dalcassians. The child's father was Kennedy (Ceinnéidigh in Irish), son of Lorcan. Kennedy was a *bó-aire*, or cattle lord, possessing a wealth of fine black cattle. Kennedy's wife, who was called Bebinn, was the daughter of a king of West Connacht, another *bó-aire*.

Elected as a king of Thomond, Lorcan was the first of his tribe to lead an army outside his own territory. He once claimed the right to be king of all Munster but his claim was hotly contested by the more powerful Munster tribe, the Owenachts, and eventually he and his followers were defeated. They never forgot.

By the time Brian was born, Kennedy and Bebinn already had eleven sons. Such large families were common: it was important to have many children in order to be certain of raising at least a few. When Brian was born most if not all of his brothers were still alive, as were an impressive number of aunts and uncles and cousins.

Kennedy's home was an Iron Age ringfort known as Béal Boru, on the west bank of the Shannon River in what is now County Clare. Thomond at that time was heavily forested; some referred to it as a wilderness. Majestic red deer as large as horses stalked the heights, like kings surveying their realms. Dense woodlands were home to shy but beautiful pine martens, with fur of glossy chocolate brown, a bushy tail and dazzlingly white throat. A dawn chorus of songbirds greeted the sunrise; a sleepy nocturne announced the fall of night.

From Béal Boru one could see the southern bay of Lough Derg in one direction and the purple and brown mountains of Craglea and Thountinna in the other. The southern slope of Craglea was home to Ayvinn (Aoibhinn), the traditional banshee of the Dalcassians. On the flank of the mountain, a well sacred to Ayvinn gushed from a cleft in the crag. According to legend, the banshee's appearance always signalled the death of a chief of the tribe.

The Dalcassians had once been important in Munster, but tribal warfare had taken its toll. By the time Brian was born they had subsided into near-obscurity, yearning for lost glories. They could have disappeared from history without leaving a trace, except for a curious quirk in the nature of Kennedy's youngest son: Brian mac Kennedy was unwilling to accept limitations.

Brian was the sort of boy who throws a stone into the water just to see how far the ripples will go. While still a small child he had listened with fascination to the tales that visiting storytellers told beside the fire. Such storytellers were an important part of Gaelic life, the entertainment that made dark winter nights bearable. Their repertoire invariably included the great heroic tales: Nuada of the Silver Arm; Cúchulainn, the invincible warrior; Fionn Mac Cumhaill, the outlaw leader of the Fianna.

Inspired by these legends, when he was little more than a toddler Brian taught himself to use the dagger and the casting spear. Because he was the youngest of his family, there was a shortage of boys his own age to take part in his games. He had to invent his enemies. As he grew older he lost interest in pretend battles against shadowy opponents and began to dream of adulthood, with its own set of fantasies and ambitions. But the early tales and first heroes of a child become permanent fixtures in the mind.

Brehon law decreed an education to be the birthright of the noble class. Brian's parents might have intended him for the priesthood as every Christian family sought to give at least one son to God. But his brother Marcan, seventh in the line of Kennedy's sons, already was showing a strong preference for the Church. When Marcan entered a monastery young Brian was sent too to study at the great monastic centres of Clonmacnois and Inisfallen. These were staffed by highly educated monks who had studied throughout Europe. Under their strict tutelage Brian learned to read Greek and Latin. He memorised the careers of Caesar and Charlemagne, studied the tactics of Xenophon's cavalry and the deployment of the naval fleet of Xerxes. His mind was like a sponge, thirstily soaking up information.

When Brian was ten years old his father was killed in battle by Callahan of the Owenacht tribe. Several of Brian's brothers suffered a similar fate. Four years after Kennedy's death, Brian's oldest surviving brother, Mahon, acceded to their father's title as king of Thomond.

It was a kingship lacking much in the way of power or royal prerogatives, but this probably suited Mahon, who was not a warrior by nature but a kindly, gentle man. He preferred negotiation to confrontation as a way of protecting his tribe.

Unfortunately, confrontation was the way things were achieved in Ireland. In 959 the Owenacht king of Munster died and another prince of his tribe, a man called Molloy, declared himself king and set up court at Cashel.

During the years when Brian was occupied with his studies, Mahon followed the path of expediency. He began trading with the Norse settlers along the Shannon, who bought the furs of seal, otter, badger and fox from the Dalcassians. Mahon made a number of concessions to those same settlers in order to keep peace. Inevitably, he quarrelled with his youngest brother, who had now completed his education. Brian saw everything in black and white; as far as he was concerned Mahon was a traitor. While still in his late teens Brian broke with his brother completely. Gathering a company of young, like-minded followers, he struck out into the mountains of east Clare to fight the foreigners on his own terms.

His little band was clothed in coarse homespun wool or in deer hide and often went barefoot. Their weapons included the iron-bladed Irish axe – a basic, multi-purpose implement equally suited to domestic use – and the javelin. Belted around their waists was a thrusting sword. When their weapons were damaged they learned to repair them themselves. They fashioned circular shields out of wood. They used both their spears and the bow and arrow in order to live off the land, hunting wild boar in the forest and brown hare on the meadows, spearing fish in the rivers, trapping badgers and weasels as they emerged from their dens. They even collected bats from their caves if all else failed. Of necessity, the young rebels learned to eat almost anything.

Around their necks they wore leather bags containing a day's provisions of dried meat and hazelnuts. If they were lucky, they might be given a bit of hard cheese by some sympathetic herder. They became very tough and very resilient. They were warriors.

Lightly armed and lightly equipped, Brian's band was a highly mobile force. They were well able to swoop down from the hills and fall on their enemies. Their traditional method of warfare, inherited from their Celtic ancestors, was to rush forward in no particular order and try to overcome the enemy by sheer force. The side with numerical superiority usually won.

At first the Irish were almost exterminated by powerfully built Norse husbands and fathers who had better weapons. After the initial shock, Brian responded by introducing his band to a code of discipline which he had gleaned from his classical studies. His ideas must have seemed incomprehensible to the young rebels. He realised they could not count on numerical superiority because they did not have it. There had to be another way to win. There was: he discovered within himself a gift for tactical ingenuity. A careful study of the annals reveals that Brian Boru mastered the art of guerrilla warfare long before the term was invented.

He learned to use the land itself as a weapon. Opponents could be tricked into floundering into a bog and drowning. Or lured into a steep defile where they could not find a way out. Brian soon knew every treacherous piece of ground in Thomond and how best to exploit it. He relied on the element of surprise, striking without mercy and then vanishing back into the trackless mountains he knew so well. Most battles were fought in the daytime, but he was not afraid to attack at night. When he stood no chance of winning, he retreated rather than make a heroic but futile last stand, which would cost the lives of his men.

Brian put a stop to the mindless, headlong charge practised by the Gael by insisting on drilling his troops. Perhaps he even tied the legs of pairs of men together as they marched, as was reported by early chroniclers. His followers may not have liked his methods at first, but they learned to respect him. They also learned to follow orders without question, knowing there was a plan behind them.

The Norse, whose traditional way of battle was similar to the reckless charge of the Gael, were confused by these tactics.

Sometime during this period Brian captured a Viking battle-axe. Short-hafted, broad-socketed, intended to be clasped with both hands to give more power to the swing, the so-called Lochlann axe was deadly in hand-to-hand fighting. Brian took his into a stand of young ash saplings and taught himself to use it. Swinging with all his weight behind it, until he thought the muscles of his shoulders and upper arms would tear free from his bones.

The Viking axe was a singularly savage weapon. While a sword might kill a man outright if very skilfully wielded, it was more likely to cause a wound that would gradually prove fatal, either through loss of blood or a subsequent infection. But one powerful blow from a Viking axe could extinguish life within a heartbeat.

Exceptional energy and his genius for strategy were enough to sustain Brian for almost two years. Poets were beginning to sing of him in royal halls, which was the ultimate tribute to a warrior, but he was losing his followers to attrition. Men he cared about poured out their life's blood onto stony soil. Meanwhile Mahon's policies were rewarding members of his tribe with food in the bowl and fat on the knife. No new young Dalcassians arrived to join the outlaws in the hills.

Their second winter in the wilds was bitterly cold. Ice formed on the Shannon. A savage wind from the Atlantic blew incessantly across Thomond, until no birds would fly. There was no game to be speared and eaten, even the vermin had disappeared underground. Brian's companions were reduced to gnawing roots dug out of the frozen soil, but these did not provide enough nourishment to sustain a fighting man. For shelter they constructed rude huts made of branches. The wind tore through this meagre protection and chilled sleeping men to the bone, so they awakened shivering and feverish.

It was hard to admit defeat. The foreigners did not beat Brian, he told himself. The weather did.

A headstrong and rebellious youth had stormed off into the wilderness. Eighteen months later a haggard, exhausted, but wiser man returned, accompanied by the surviving handful of his warrior band. They were gaunt and hollow-eyed and staggered as they walked, but their heads were held high. When Brian led them into Mahon's hall they brought with them the scent of the wilderness.

Their fellow Dalcassians stared. Even dressed in rags, Brian of Béal Boru must have been memorable. His contemporaries described him as being exceptionally tall. Julius Caesar had written of the Gaulish Celts, 'They are taller by the length of a man's forearm than the tallest of my legions.' According to anthropologists, the Irish Celts produced large, well built men and women. It would take famine to shrink them to small stature; generations of improved nutrition are reversing the process. Brian also may have been red-haired. The gene for red hair which was almost ubiquitous with the Celts, was common among the Irish, and greatly admired; now it is slowly disappearing throughout the world.

Overjoyed at his brother's return, Mahon urged Brian to join him and settle down. He may even have suggested a princess of Connacht who would make a fine wife for him. Brian was not averse to the idea of marrying – he was the age for marrying – but he had no intention of settling down. In front of the other Dalcassians he angrily accused his brother of abandoning the inheritance of their ancestors and surrendering their sovereignty to foreigners. We do not know exactly what Brian said to Mahon, but it was the first known example of a gift for powerful oratory that would transform his life. Sometime during that speech Mahon felt the weight of opinion shift against him. Perhaps against his better judgement, he agreed to call an assembly of the chieftains of Thomond. When Brian addressed them the result was unanimous. War! As with one voice, the clan leaders voted to attack the foreigners and expel them from their seats of power.

With his firebrand brother by his side, Mahon mac Kennedy set out to claim the prize which had escaped their father: the kingship of the province of Munster. This was an act of blatant defiance to Ivar, the Norse king of Limerick, who had allied himself with the Owenacht princes. During this period the indefatigable Brian also found time to marry Mor, a princess of Connacht and daughter of a powerful petty king. Mor would bear him three sons – Murrough, Conor, and Flann – and at least one daughter. Brian's followers referred to them as 'the cubs of the lion'.

Although Mahon was the nominal commander of the Dalcassian army, it was Brian who led the allied tribes against Ivar of Limerick in 967. After winning a spectacular victory at the battle of Sulcoit in what is now county Limerick, he pursued the Norsemen back to their stronghold and set fire to the town. A fortune in Viking plunder, including gold jewellery and silver-trimmed saddles set with precious gems, was retrieved

and shared out among the victors. The Norse who survived the catastrophe crept off into the hills to hide from
the fury of Brian Boru. And the stories about him spread.

The ruling Owenacht tribe, traditional enemy of the
Dalcassians, was dismayed by this unexpected consolida-
tion of power in Munster. For once, Gaelic chieftains
were not fighting amongst themselves, but had united
to turn their full force on the foreigners. Such a policy
could seriously threaten the autonomy of petty kings
like Molloy. It must be stopped. But among the Gael, the
impetus of victory was unstoppable and finally Owenacht
power was replaced by Dalcassian. Mahon mac Kennedy
was acclaimed as king of Munster.

His inauguration took place on the Rock of Cashel,
Ireland's Acropolis. On this site St Patrick had converted
a sixth-century pagan king to Christianity. Since that
time the Rock had been not only royal but holy, the perfect place for kingmaking. With a gold circlet resting on
his brow, Mahon was content at last: he had achieved the
height of his ambition. His clan and tribe were restored
to their rightful status. His father could sleep peacefully
in his grave.

For young Brian, the inauguration at the Rock of
Cashel was certainly not a final achievement. Rather, it
would be a stepping stone.

Under his leadership the army of Munster repeatedly repelled invading war parties from Leinster. Leinster was the most contentious of the provinces, comprised of tribes who constantly battled one another for supremacy, battles which spilled over into other territories. Arrogant, given to snobbery and loving intrigue, the Leinstermen kept their own province in a state of upheaval and their neighbours in Munster on edge. There was no love lost between the two provinces.

Brian was both an inspiring leader of men and a clever tactician who won more often than he lost. With Brian holding the Leinstermen at bay – more or less – Mahon was able to hold court in style atop the Rock of Cashel. Kings were expected to dispense unlimited hospitality as well as make just judgements when called upon to do so. Mahon excelled at both. Most of his people loved him. But envy and belligerence ran deep. Other Munster princes desired his crown. The Owenacht, in particular, deeply resented what they saw as a usurpation of their ancient right to rule.

In 976 Mahon was assassinated through a conspiracy which involved Molloy, self-proclaimed king of the Owenachts, and Donovan, a prince of the Desmond tribe, as well as Ivar, the bitter ex-king of Limerick. Brian took the death of his beloved brother very hard. The guilty

Owenacht and Desmonian princes were tracked down and slain. Molloy died at the hands of Brian's young son Murrough.

At one time, this would have signalled a bloody feud that would last for generations and inspire countless poets. But by now Brian was thirty-five years old. If marriage and fatherhood had not tamed the lion, at least they had given him a sense of the future. After cornering Ivar on an island in the Shannon and killing him with his bare hands, Brian allowed his Norsemen to retain Limerick in return for an annual tribute of wine. This unexpectedly generous gesture would bear fruit in years to come when former Vikings began to think of themselves as Irishmen.

On the strength of his military achievements Brian Boru was chosen by acclaim to follow his dead brother as king of Munster. By the autumn of 976 he occupied the royal stronghold atop Cashel. Thus began a reign unique in the Irish annals for its achievements.

In Ireland a plethora of ancient laws laid down specific prohibitions for every king. At his inauguration Brian would have sworn to observe those binding the monarch of Cashel. He was forbidden to hold a court before celebrating the feast of Loch Lein; to spend a wet autumn night before winter in Letrecha; to camp for nine days on the River Suir; to hold a meeting at the boundary near

Gowran; and to hear the complaints of oppressed women on the plain between Cashel and Clonmel. Each of these taboos undoubtedly dated back to some misfortune that had once befallen a king of Munster.

Conversely, Brian had to promise to obey the orders demanded of his kingship, namely to despoil Cruachan at the call of the cuckoo; to burn the Laighin to the north of Gabair; to chant the Lenten prayers at Cashel; to cross the Knockmealdown Mountains after pacifying the south of Ireland; and to lead a dark grey army across the plains of north Carlow and south Kildare – on a Tuesday. It had to be a Tuesday.

This is but a small example of the countless laws, rules and superstitions that shaped the lives of the Gael in the tenth century, each a remnant of the ancient past.

Brian would spend the next twenty-two years reorganising and consolidating Munster by alternately punishing and persuading its tribes to make them submit to his authority. To the astonishment of everyone, Brian promised his young daughter Sabia – identified by some annalists as Sive – in marriage to his old Owenacht enemy Molloy's oldest son, Cian. Cian was said to exceed all other men in stature and beauty, and would prove to be a valuable ally for his father-in-law. Cian was instrumental in effecting a truce between rival princes of the

Owenacht and Desmond tribes, whose quarrels were keeping Munster unsettled. A few years later Cian joined Brian in forcing the submission of the Norse king of Waterford.

In order to enforce submission from another king, battle was not always necessary. A common and more popular method was the taking of hostages, which often could be achieved through intimidation or even stealth. The higher in rank these hostages were, the more eager – in theory – their tribe would be to get them back. But hospitality was of paramount importance in the Gaelic world and a man's prestige was seriously at risk if he failed to be a magnanimous host. Any king who took hostages was obliged to treat them well and provide them with the best accommodations and the finest food and drink, better than that served at his own table, if possible. Taking too many hostages had ruined more than one king, when his 'guests' simply refused to go home.

Brian took a large number of hostages during his time at Cashel. An ever-expanding cluster of guesting houses surrounded the base of the Rock, forming the foundations of what would some day be a sizeable town. When their tribes sent the requested tribute to the king of Munster the hostages were released without question. The annalists kept no record of how many refused to return home, but surely some did. Throughout his life Brian Boru would be a generous host.

He used a third of the tributes he received to build roads, drain boglands, and repair churches and monasteries that had been damaged by Irish raiders as well as by Viking marauders. He also sent emissaries abroad to find and bring back treasures which the Vikings had stolen. In this manner Brian rescued a number of priceless artefacts 'from damp and Danes'. This was probably arranged with the assistance of his secretary, Maolsuthain Ua Cearbhaill (O'Carroll), a well travelled, highly educated man who had connections on the continent of Europe and would remain with Brian all his life.

After summoning a convocation of the foremost judges and kings to Cashel, Brian personally worked with them to reinterpret Irish law based on the *Psalter of Cashel*. This psalter had originated with St Benean, a disciple of St Patrick, and contained the original record of the tributes of Munster – what was owed to the king and when it was to be paid, all organised under the patronage of the Church. In the ninth century it had been amended by Cormac mac Cuilleanáin, archbishop of Cashel, and included a reference to the fact that the king of Ulster had the collecting of all milk and sewing thread in his province, and other such details. Under Brian Boru's guidance it was rewritten again and expanded to conform to the needs of his time. Parts of this work still exist in the much later *Book of Rights*.

During this period Brian also modified his own marital arrangements. In accordance with Brehon law, which allowed a man to have more than one wife if he could afford to care for her, Brian married Achra, a princess of Meath, whose father was a tributary king of the southern branch of the powerful Uí Néill tribe. In time, several children were born to Brian and Achra, including two sons, Domnall and Tadhg.

The annalists make no mention of the reaction of the Christian clergy to this marriage, but one may assume they were not pleased. However, Brian was quite able to ignore the censure of others when it served his purpose. Heaven could wait. Bit by bit, he was patching something else together.

The Ireland he knew was a fractured emerald, divided and subdivided by provinces and tribes and endless petty quarrels. The arrival of the Vikings had exacerbated the fault lines. As if that were not enough, the island was also divided into two halves, Leth Cuin in the north and Leth Moga in the south, in a tradition dating back to the coming of the Gael at the dawn of the Iron Age. The borders between north and south were always relatively fluid, depending upon which chieftains were in the ascendancy. The Uí Néill were the dominant tribe, over-lords of both halves. From their stronghold at Aileach, in what is now county Donegal, Uí Néill princes claimed tribute from the north. Their southern seat of power was at Tara, in county Meath, where their monopoly of the high kingship and the tribute of the southern provinces seemed as fixed as the stars.

But why should it be?

In 980 the title of Árd Rí was assumed by Malachy Mór, whose father was a prince of the northern Uí Néill; he also was qualified on his mother's side to hold the kingship of the southern Uí Néill – the tribe to which Brian's new wife was related. His marriage to Achra had linked Brian with the most powerful tribe in Ireland. Such connections were of paramount importance in determining rank and prestige, which is why the bards had spent decades memorising genealogies long before the arrival of literacy.

Malachy was well equipped to be a king. In addition to considerable physical strength and a good character, he was an exceptional horsemen. He took pride in being able to manage a stallion that had never been ridden or handled in any way until it was seven years old. It was said that the first time he mounted such an animal he could ride it as any other man would ride an old tame mare.

Almost from the day of his inauguration at Tara, Malachy was at war. Under the rule of Olaf Cuaran, known as 'Olaf of the Sandals', the king of Dublin, the city had acquired a black name for the number and ill-treatment of its Irish captives. To make matters worse, Olaf Cuaran had formed an alliance with Donall, king of the neighbouring province of Leinster. Together they were ravaging the royal territory of Meath. Malachy Mór gathered his new army and set out to teach them a lesson they would never forget.

Olaf Cuaran had ruled Dublin for more than a generation. During that time he had converted to Christianity and encouraged his followers to join him. Most of the Dublin Danes had become at least nominal Christians, though for some their pagan tendencies died hard. By 980 Olaf Cuaran was worn and tired. He had outlived two wives, participated in a number of battles, and in his later years had married again. She was Gormlaith, princess of Leinster. The aging king had been proud when his very young and very beautiful new wife bore him a son, whom they called Sitric. But those may have been his last days of happiness.

Marriage to Gormlaith was like trying to sail a small

boat in a tempest. She could not resist causing trouble. If there was no conspiracy afoot to keep her entertained, she concocted one. While she was in the royal palace in Dublin there was never any peace for an old man. When Olaf Cuaran and his Leinster allies were soundly whipped in battle by Malachy, the newly crowned Árd Rí, Olaf surrendered to the inevitable. He may have been reluctant to give up his kingship but he was not unhappy to turn his back on his marriage. He abandoned both Dublin and Gormlaith and fled to a monastery. The one he chose had been founded by St Columba in 563, on the island of Iona; it is believed that the famous illuminated Book of Kells, now in Trinity College, Dublin, was begun on Iona but later removed to Kells in Ireland.

Iona was part of a sixth-century Irish settlement which once had included Argyll on the Scottish mainland and the islands of the Hebrides. The settlers were members of the Dal Riada tribe in northern Ireland. Their descendants were the highland Scots, who for centuries would resist English domination with indomitable courage. The monastery St Columba founded on Iona had been a frequent target of the Vikings. Perhaps Olaf Cuaran went there as an act of contrition, but if so, he did not have much time to gain forgiveness. Not long after his arrival on Iona, the old king died.

Upon payment of an exorbitantly high tribute, Malachy Mór allowed Sitric, who was so young they still called him 'Silkbeard', to succeed his father as king of Dublin. He was not the first king of Dublin to bear that name; at least three had preceded him over the years: 'Sigtryggr' was a popular Viking name. The arrangement was somewhat reminiscent of Brian Boru's generous treatment of the Norse in Limerick, but it did not win the eternal loyalty of the Danes of Dublin for Malachy. Their allegiance was given to their new king and through him to his uncle, Maelmora of Leinster, Gormlaith's brother.

Sitric, and thus Maelmora, were now connected to one of the most prosperous trading confederations in the world. The collapse of the Roman Empire in the fifth century had meant the end of a great merchant network, but in time the Vikings constructed something similar to suit themselves. By the late tenth century they were trading with rising commercial interests along the borders of the English Channel and the North Sea. The once-flourishing traffic in luxury goods through the Mediterranean was long gone, but now Swedish and Danish adventurers were opening new trade routes from Byzantium to Russia, and importing eastern goods to the northern coasts.

Dublin had become a very valuable property. Sitric and Maelmora looked upon it as their own. Let the new Árd Rí have the rest of Ireland – ancient, backward Ireland.

Malachy Mór did not see it that way. He set about confirming his new position by demanding tribute from the provincial kings. The Uí Néill of Ulster responded immediately, as he expected. Connacht took a little longer, and Leinster longer still, sending only a fraction of the cattle due a high king.

Nothing was heard from Munster.

By this time Malachy was well aware of the rise to power of Brian Boru. From Malachy's point of view the Dalcassian upstart lacked the credentials to be a provincial king at all. To remind him what real power was, Malachy led an army to Thomond to cut down the inaugural tree of the Dalcassians, the sacred oak beneath which every king of Thomond was crowned. This gesture of domi-nance was something the Dalcassian at Cashel could hardly ignore. Malachy fully expected that the Munster tribute would arrive at Tara in due course. Things had always been done this way in Ireland.

The Árd Rí then marched into Leinster to attack its king, Donall, take a number of hostages and destroy most of his army. Malachy ordered his men to collect double the number of cattle still due to him and deliver them to his personal fort at Dun na Sciath – the Fort of the Shield – on Lough Ennell, in what is now County Westmeath. The high king's army swept through the green countryside driving everything before it, including all the cattle from the royal stronghold of Naas, which was surrounded by some of the richest grassland in Ireland. Maelmora, senior among the princes living at Naas, was one of those left to pick up the pieces.

Maelmora was a man with his own agenda. He aspired to the kingship of the province, and saw the defeat of the pious Donall as a step in the right direction. Although he was seething inside over the loss of the royal herds, Maelmora did not openly defy the new Árd Rí. Politics triumphed over passion. He played his trump card. One might more accurately say he played his queen.

Chess was an extremely popular game in Ireland. The Gaelic version of this almost universal game was known as *fidchell,* and was the perfect pastime when inclement weather kept warriors from taking the field. No chieftain worthy of the gold torc he wore around his neck would fail to have at least one board and a set of chessmen among his possessions. The *fidchell* board was carved from yew wood and divided into black and white squares. The chessmen were two and a half inches tall, elaborately carved and embellished with precious metals. Chess furniture was considered so much of a necessity that it was classified along with food under Brehon law. Brian Boru's favourite chess pieces were said to be fashioned entirely of yellow gold and white bronze, and the soft leather bag in which they were stored was gilded. Maelmora of Leinster considered himself a champion at chess.

In 984 Maelmora encouraged Malachy Mór to marry his sister, the newly widowed princess Gormlaith, former wife of Olaf Cuaran. Maelmora assured Malachy that the marriage would be sufficient to gain the loyalty of himself and his followers among the Leinstermen. In addition, through Gormlaith's son, Sitric, the commercial strength of Dublin would be at the disposal of the high king. Last but not least – and Maelmora did not mention this to Malachy – having family ties with the Árd Rí should help strengthen Maelmora's own claim to the kingship of Leinster.

Everyone involved thought it was a wonderful idea. Almost everyone; history does not record Gormlaith's opinion in the matter. Her opinions would only become important later.

Malachy's marriage was motivated by something more than politics. In spite of having a son old enough to be king of Dublin, Gormlaith was still famed for her beauty.

The poets claimed she had the neck of a swan and hair so long it brushed her ankles. At the very least, she was memorable. Satisfied that he had established his authority beyond question, Malachy took his trophy wife home to Dun na Sciath and began entertaining Gaelic nobility in the style expected of an Árd Rí.

He had made a bad mistake in judgement. Or perhaps two.

Following the destruction of the inaugural tree of the Dalcassians, Brian Boru had begun to gather a fleet of longships. His generosity to the Norsemen of Limerick after the death of Ivar was not forgotten, and a number of them not only provided ships but served as crewmen. While Malachy was feasting on swans and wild boar and showing off his new wife, Brian was sailing up the Shannon. He marched an army into Meath and laid waste great swathes of land before the distracted Árd Rí even knew he was there. Brian returned in triumph to the acclaim of Munster, which paid no tribute to Tara that year. Or for many years to come.

Brian continued to strengthen his position through calculated diplomacy as well as a subtle show of strength. He called upon Munster's petty kings and princes, one by one. Where possible he established friendly relations with each of them. On one or two occasions he took hostages, however, hostages whom he treated with the same exemplary hospitality as always. When their tribes furnished the required tribute they were promptly released, though some preferred to stay with Brian Boru.

He widened his round of visits to include the kings and princes of the other noble families in the southern provinces, including recalcitrant Leinster. Accompanied by an impressive retinue of well-equipped warriors, purely for show he insisted, he presented his peers with generous gifts for themselves and their families, and gave large endowments to their churches and schools.

By the end of the tenth century Brian Boru considered himself not only king of Munster, but ruler of all Leth Moga. What followed was inevitable.

CHAPTER THREE

VIKINGS

Stern land breeds strong men. The inhabitants of the countries now known as Norway, Denmark and Sweden were a hardy breed accustomed to surviving in a cold climate with few natural resources. Subsistence farming was difficult at best. Norway was the most sterile of the territories, with too many peasants trying to farm too little soil. An early Norse historian wrote, 'All that man may use for pasture or plough lieth against the sea, and even this is in some places very rocky.'

The one limitless resource these people possessed was the sea. They made the most of it. Around 700 BC the ridden horse had given the Celts the freedom and mobility to leave their homeland and settle throughout western Europe. Around AD 600 Norse boat builders had developed a keel which allowed their boats to travel the open sea, thus making possible their territorial expansion.

The last decade of the eighth century was marked by armed raids around the coasts of Britain. The first Viking attacks were on Christian monasteries within sight of the sea. Lightweight longships with dragonheaded prows arrived with the tide and swiftly disgorged warriors of terrifying aspect. They came ashore dressed in furs and swinging battle axes, and howling for plunder. The monasteries were an easy target for them. The monks had no weapons with which to protect themselves, only scythes for cutting grass and some kitchen knives. They were humble men who lived very simply. But their small stone churches contained items of great beauty and great value. Gold or silver chalices were set with gemstones; patens were often of gold, the crosses and crosiers were works of art. The highest expression of the craftsman's art was the sacred object given to God.

Beginning in 793 with the tiny island of Lindisfarne, the spiritual heart of the British kingdom of Northumbria, the Vikings initiated a reign of terror. They seized the sacred valuables and slaughtered the peaceful monks who tried to stop them. According to the scholar Alcuin, a Northumbrian advisor to Charlemagne, 'The Church of St Cuthbert was spattered with the blood of the priests of God and despoiled of all its ornaments, a place more venerable than all in Britain is given as prey to pagan peoples.'

The shock was felt throughout Christendom.

By the end of the eighth century the Viking tide reached Ireland. The year 795 saw the first Viking attack. Their target was Lambay Island, which was then called Rechru, a small island within sight of the present-day town of Skerries, north of Dublin. St Columba had founded a monastery on Rechru and by this period the monastic community had accrued enough wealth to be a tempting target. The Viking attack followed the usual pattern: assault, murder, pillage. Perhaps one or two battered monks lived long enough to tell what had happened to them, long enough to horrify the local fishermen who found them.

The terror such incidents inspired is captured in an ancient Irish poem dated to that era:

> Fierce is the wind tonight,
> It ploughs up the white hair of the sea
> I have no fear that the Viking hosts
> Will come over the water to me.

As the Viking attacks became more frequent, the Irish became increasingly alarmed. At first the foreigners limited their raids to island communities inhabited by monks who offered no resistance. But inevitably, larger expeditions were fitted out to venture onto the mainland, burning and plundering as they came. In 812 a full-scale invasion in the region of the Lakes of Killarney was met, and defeated, by the rulers of the Gaelic tribe of the Owenacht. According to the Annals of Eginhard, who was Charlemagne's tutor, 'After no small number of the Northmen had been slain, they basely took to flight and returned home.'

They came again. And again. From 823 to 832 there is an almost unbroken record of wanton destruction. But those who began as robbers were slowly changing.

The northern lands were not rich in natural resources. Their craftsmen were skilled woodcarvers and metalworkers, but these required raw materials which were scarce at best. Foreign trade was sorely needed to supply the shortcomings of their home territory and improve the lives of its inhabitants.

Ireland, on the other hand, was abundantly supplied with oakwood forests, valuable metal ores, and fat cattle grazing on rich grasslands. Oak was highly prized for shipbuilding. Irish gold was treasured throughout Christendom. Cattle were an invaluable source of leather and tallow, which commanded high prices and could be shipped anywhere. To a shrewd commercial eye, Ireland was a warehouse waiting to be emptied.

Scandinavian traders started to visit the Irish coast, scouting for suitable locations. Waterford in the southeast and Limerick in the west were among their first discoveries. Establishing seaports around the island had never occurred to the natives. During the so-called Dark Ages students from the European continent had flocked to Ireland to study at the great monastic centres, yet the Irish had never followed up on these links to develop a commercial trading network of their own.

In 837 a fleet of Norse longships sailed into Dublin Bay, fleeing a storm. They stayed only long enough to mend their ships, but they liked what they saw. Four years later the foreigners were back in earnest. Crews of Norsemen dragged their ships ashore at a natural harbour called the Black Pool – 'Dubh Linn', in Irish – where the River Poddle entered the River Liffey before both merged with the bay. The pool was overlooked by a stone monastery on a well-drained ridge fifty feet above the highest point of the incoming tide. (Centuries later, when the city of Dublin received its first charter under the English, its name, as still preserved in the Corporation archives, was listed as 'Diveline', the English equivalent of Dubh Linn.)

The small monastery relied on a nearby Christian community for its temporal needs. A few modest huts and several tiny workshops clustered beside the ford nearest to the mouth of the River Liffey. Known as the Hurdle Ford, this marked the juncture of several ancient roads. The villagers used the ford to drive their cattle safely across the river so they could graze on the lush fields of the northern bank.

The ford's construction was uniquely Gaelic. Panels of woven wickerwork known as hurdles were thrown into the river and staked in place. When enough were piled up they provided relatively safe footing for man and beast. Because hurdles were easily constructed from local materials and easily replaced when they disintegrated, the Gael used them for many building purposes. Baile Átha Cliath – 'the town at the ford of the hurdles' – was the Irish name for the tiny community.

The Northmen did not consider the Liffey swamp a tempting site for colonising, but no harbour on the eastern coast of Ireland offered better access to the sea, so they simply took it over. Any resistance offered by the natives was overcome by force.

The Norse erected a timber stockade on the ridge and set about building a ship-fort from which they could operate on a permanent basis. When the first colonists arrived from Scandinavia they named their new settlement for the Black Pool: Dubh Linn. The former inhabitants of Baile Átha Cliath may have tried to resist, but Ireland was an underpopulated island rich in natural resources. There was room enough for all. Or so it seemed. The annals of the period express it best: 'The whole sea continued to vomit foreigners into Erin.'

If the Irish political situation was chaotic, that of the Vikings was no less so. Their homelands were divided into countless small fiefdoms. Kings and jarls battled one another for any scrap of fertile earth. Competition between the tribes was equally fierce. Any strongman who possessed a couple of longships and the loyalty of thirty-six men to crew them could become an independent entrepreneur. In time, the Vikings would build an enviable trade network that extended as far east as Russia.

In 852 a swarm of Danes descended upon Dublin, attacked the Norse and plundered their fortress. Soon afterwards the two forces fought one another at Carlingford, where the Norse were again defeated, but just barely. After this the two appeared to develop a temporary détente. In 857 the first recorded king of Dublin, a Norseman called Olaf the White, joined forces with a Danish warrior known as Ivarr the Boneless to attack

Scotland and Northumbria, where they gained a valuable foothold.

After Olaf was killed in battle, Ivarr assumed leadership both of the Norse in Ireland and the Danes in Northumbria, who were centred in York. The streets of York, originally laid out in a Roman-style grid, were being replaced by curving lanes more to the Viking taste. But Ivarr did not much care for York. Instead he undertook to create a royal seat for himself and a stronghold for his fellow Danes in Dublin. The original Viking ship-fort offered both a fine harbour and a more salubrious climate than Northumbria. At Ivarr's behest extensive work was done along the Liffey estuary to facilitate ship landings, including the construction of a strong earthen bank topped with a reinforced timber palisade. Dublin was on its way to becoming a commercial seaport.

At the centre of the growing Danish town, Ivarr the Boneless built a timber palace for himself – dark and smoky and malodorous – which he filled with looted treasure. He also constructed a Thingmote: a high mound of earth traditionally used by the Scandinavians for their parliament, which was known as the Thing. The Dublin Thingmote occupied what is now College Green. King Henry II of England met the Irish chieftains there in 1172 and held a festival at Christmas to entertain them.

The Thingmote continued to be a prominent feature of the city until 1685, when Dublin Corporation granted the Bishop of Meath a licence to destroy the historic mound and use its earth to fill the channels and create Nassau Street.

In spite of his improvements for the city, Ivarr the Boneless continued to have a restless soul. Not content with making himself a king in Ireland, Ivarr sailed off to England to join 'the great heathen army' which was terrorising that land. When he died in 873 he was buried, according to the chronicles of the era, 'in a manner befitting former times'.

Thanks to the highway of the sea, the reach of the Scandinavians was being extended. When Norse raiding parties first visited the Western Isles – a broad designation applied to numerous underpopulated islands around the western and northern fringes of Scotland – they recognised an opportunity. There was not a lot of wealth to plunder in places that could barely support their few inhabitants, but there was empty land for the taking. Land! Upon returning to their home ports the raiders reported what they had discovered. They could hardly talk about anything else. Men with the light of adventure in their eyes gazed eagerly out to sea, imagining ...

The Norwegian king, Harald the Fair-haired, decided

to add the islands to his territorial acquisitions. One group in particular attracted his interest. The Orkneys consist of more than seventy islands and islets twenty miles north of the Scottish mainland. Some are habitable, some are not. Some are too small for anything but seabirds. Humans have dwelt among these islands since the Stone Age. Skara Brae is one of the most complete Neolithic settlements in Europe.

The Orkneys are virtually treeless and have little arable soil, but there was enough on the largest island, or mainland, to sustain a Norse stronghold, though they would have to import timber for shipbuilding. The mainland was mostly low and undulating, with good trout fishing in its streams. From the Viking point of view its greatest asset was the extensive landlocked harbour called Scapa Flow. The main entrance is in the south, where it opens onto Pentland Firth, the strait that separates the Orkneys from the Scottish mainland. There are also channels leading to the North Sea on the east and the Atlantic on the west. During both World Wars the British fleet was stationed at Scapa Flow. In short, the Orkneys were an ideal home base for Vikings.

Harald the Fair-Haired appointed his brother Sigurd to rule as earl of Orkney. Harald also named a ruler for the Hebrides: a wild warrior called Ketil Flatnose. With his king in distant Norway, Flatnose was free to do just as he liked. It was a great time for opportunists. Subsequent island warlords ruled like kings themselves; most notably Earl Sigurd the Second, better known as Sigurd the Stout, whose triumphant career would come to a sudden and painful end at the Battle of Clontarf.

The first Vikings in Ireland had not ventured far inland, lacking the organisation to attempt a conquest of the entire island. The sea was their element and so for a while they had stayed within earshot of it. But farming was also part of their heritage. In time the former sea rovers took up the plough. Their first farming communities were set up around their ports: Waterford and Wexford, Limerick and Carlingford. As trade expanded, political alliances were forged. The strongest and most enduring of these would be in Leinster. Christianity still co-existed with paganism in Ireland, so it seemed possible that Gael and Northman might enjoy a similar relationship.

Not everyone was convinced. With increasing hostility, Gaelic chieftains in other parts of Ireland resisted foreign incursions into their land – although as Brian Boru would later observe, many Irish children were born with Norse-silver hair and sea-green eyes.

As Dublin grew, shipwrights were in constant demand.

A fleet of Danish longships routinely harboured in the bay. Narrow lanes were lined with rows of square houses roofed with thatch. The homes of the prosperous were walled with planks thrust into the earth. Poorer folk made do with wicker, or wattle-and-daub. Timber walkways protected pedestrians from the omnipresent mud and sewage in the streets.

Cramped shops and awninged stalls bustled with haggling customers. Behind the markets, craftsmen and artisans laboured in their workshops to satisfy demand. Anything that could be bought or sold, from bare necessities to imported luxury items, from swans for the table to nubile women for the bed, was available. Jewellery made of gleaming jet or polished amber from the Baltic or colourful Egyptian glass beads brought high prices. Combs skilfully fashioned from antler horn were a more modest gift for one's woman. To provide meat for the family table, livestock was kept within the walls of Dublin and grazed on two grassy areas adjacent to the city, Fair Green to the southwest and Hoggen Green to the east. On Sandymount, below Hoggen Green, women and children searched the strand for cockles and mussels.

North of the Liffey was an expanse of broken, rolling land with occasional pockets of ash, elm and hazel. The little hazel trees were coppiced by industrious Dubliners to provide a bounteous supply of wattles for construction; the hazel nuts were a favourite food of children and goats.

The population of Dublin did not consist solely of Vikings and their descendants. Increasingly the city was used as a holding point for Irish slaves captured in battle, who were then shipped to distant seaports. A ready market in the distant east was developing for men, women and particularly children. Dublin was turning a nice profit for the Vikings.

Olaf Cuaran had become king of Dublin in 945 after losing his throne to a rival in Northumbria. He exchanged the Danish stronghold at York for a kingdom in Ireland that stretched from the monastery at Swords in the north to the trading centre at Arklow in the south, and included a fleet of ships in the Irish Sea. When Olaf was baptised most of his subjects followed him into the new religion. His son, Sitric Silkbeard, was raised as a Christian. By the end of the tenth century constant warfare with the Irish had shrunk their dominion to Dublin and its immediate environs, but the Danish city still had considerable influence.

Meath king and Árd Rí Malachy Mór's connection with the new young king of the Dublin Danes was seen as a clever move.

Ireland and Scandinavia were more alike at this time

than one might think, right down to the board games they loved to play. Both societies were rapidly becoming Christianised. The base of both cultures was agrarian and agricultural, with landholdings endlessly subdivided. Slavery made a significant contribution to the labour force. Power struggles among the ruling classes were a constant. Interludes of warfare were as frequent as the changes in the seasons. A herder on a lonely hillside or a fisherman casting his nets in the sea might be oblivious to the battles raging across the land, but most people were aware that their circumstances might change suddenly and drastically. For the ordinary man and woman life could be hard. And short. For the nobility it could be lavish ... and equally short.

At the dawn of the eleventh century the Vikings controlled not only the outlying British islands, but much of Scotland and northern England. Former 'land leapers' were settling down and consolidating their gains. Earls and princes and even kings, many of them self-appointed, were cropping up everywhere. A man like Sigurd the Stout, who boasted of direct descent from Thorfinn the Skull Splitter, was even prouder to be called the earl of Orkney.

In common with most rulers of his time, Sigurd the Stout had several wives and concubines over the years and sired a number of children. His youngest son was named Thorfinn in honour of his famous ancestor, and would be six years of age at the time of the Battle of Clontarf. Little Thorfinn was not present for the battle, but his oldest brother was.

A sometime ally of Sigurd's was called Brodir, a Danish pirate who claimed to be both prince of the Isle of Man and chief of the Danes of Denmark. Whether or not the claim was true, he did have a number of followers. Mercenaries under his command roved through the Western Isles and pillaged the coastal settlements of Britain. Brodir was famed for his savage nature and his coarse black hair, which was so long he tucked it into his belt. His was a strange story. When he was a young man Brodir had been baptised as a Christian, and even appointed a deacon in the Church. Later he had reverted to the paganism of his ancestors to accommodate the violence of his chosen way of life. It was rumoured that he also practised the dark arts of sorcery. Like Sigurd the Stout, Brodir would meet his destiny at the Battle of Clontarf.

In 1014 Dublin was ruled by Sitric Silkbeard, whose mother, Gormlaith, was living with him. Few men ever had such a mother. Of Gormlaith the poets truly said, 'She was the fairest of all women and best gifted in everything that was not in her power. She did all things ill over which she had any power.'

The Irish pronounced her name Gurmla, the Scandinavians would call her Kormlada, and commemorate her in their sagas. It would be fair to say she was Ireland's Helen of Troy.

CHAPTER FOUR

THE PRINCIPALS

ad Brian Boru operated on a larger stage or
in a different era he could have been world
famous. If he had undertaken foreign conquest he might
have been mentioned in the same breath as Caesar and
Napoleon. There is no denying he was a man of large
appetites. Four wives and a large number of children testify
to his virility, and his record in battle was unsurpassed. In
addition to physical strength he possessed a brilliant, ques-
tioning mind and an uncommon ability to see the larger
picture. On his climb to the top, Brian seems at times
to have been a giant among pygmies. He came from a
background tightly circumscribed by tradition and religion. When it was to his advantage he conformed, but he
could just as easily overthrow the old rules with one slash

of the sword and create new ones, apparently undeterred by conscience. As a leader of men he must have been mesmerising. There is no other way to account for his meteoric rise to power.

Cogadh Gaedhel re Gallaibh, which translates as 'The War of the Irish with the Foreigners', is the oldest surviving account of Brian Boru's career. It was compiled from three early manuscripts, two of which now exist only in fragmentary form, and was commissioned by Brian's great-grandson, Muirchertach Ua Briain. Some claim parts were written by Brian's trusted friend, the royal poet Mac Liag. The descriptions of the Battle of Clontarf were taken from accounts given by the survivors and handed down for two generations. Although condemned by Brian's detractors as a mere hagiography, the text is as immediate as a journalist's report from the front.

The picture it gives of Brian shows him as brilliant and unpredictable. An opportunist who understood the value of surprise, in negotiations he was cunning and patient. His military genius lay in doing things the Gael had never done before. He created the first navy in Ireland; at one time three hundred boats were moored near his stronghold on the Shannon River. He mounted his best captains on horses to increase their mobility, thus creating the first Irish cavalry, in spite of the fact that Irishmen traditionally fought on foot. Realising that there was a natural advantage to offence, he developed a network of spies. A war party expecting to take him by surprise would be alarmed to discover Brian coming to meet them and attacking first. An enemy seeking to capitalise on Brian's mistakes would be disappointed, because he never made the same one twice. He thoroughly scouted the ground before engaging in battle; if he did not like what he saw he lured his opponents to a position more advantageous for himself. The clever stratagems Brian had discovered while studying Caesar and Xenophon became part of his arsenal. As he grew older he actually fought less and less, preferring to win bloodless victories through cunning and guile.

Brian had a darker side. On occasion he was subject to violent outbursts of temper. After his victory against Ivar of Limerick, Brian not only pursued the defeated Norsemen back to their base, he ordered Ivar's dispirited warriors to be rounded up and forced to watch while his army looted at will and set fire to the town. When they found a crowd of Irish children huddled in terror – little boys and girls the Norse had kidnapped to sell as slaves – Brian ordered his men to march an equal number of their captives onto Singland ridge, near Limerick. There the hapless Norsemen were put to the sword. It was said that Brian beheaded many of them himself.

The reputation for ferocity that he gained during his early years would serve him well later, when many of his opponents preferred surrender to fighting him.

If Brian could destroy, he could also construct. He built bridges and cleared new roads in order to make it easier to concentrate his troops for attack or defense. Described by a twentieth-century military historian as 'a notable builder of forts', he erected and garrisoned substantial fortresses at Roscrea, Cahir, Bruree, and Limerick. From their extant sites we can deduce that he had a keen eye for the defendable position, as well as knowing when a location offered offensive opportunities. In addition to his military constructions he built a number of churches, including those at Killaloe, Iniscaltra and Tuamgraney.

The programme of improvements Brian began as king of Munster would continue throughout his life. Even after a thousand years, a few fragments of his many achievements remain. One is the carved stone doorway of the church at Tuamgraney, a few miles north of Killaloe. The ancient church now houses the East Clare Heritage Centre.

During these years Brian took yet another wife, Duvcholly, a daughter of Cathal Ua Connor, king of Connacht. Their marriage substantially strengthened his personal connections with the western province, whose warriors were famed for their fighting ability. By now it was obvious he was thinking very far ahead.

Brian's heart belonged on the wooded banks of the Shannon. Although as king of Munster he technically ruled from the royal seat at Cashel, he began building a permanent, well-fortified residence very near, if not actually incorporating, the old ringfort of his childhood at Béal Boru.

Brian called his new stronghold Kincora – *Ceann Coradh* in Irish, translated as 'The Head of the Weir'. Kincora took its name from the old fishing weir below Béal Boru. Weirs were openwork cages built around oak stakes and placed in a stream as a trap for eels and river fish. Properly bedded deep in the streambed, weirs might last for many years. In view of the future, it seems almost prescient that Brian chose to name his residence for one.

For the rest of his life Brian Boru would rule from his palace at Kincora, no matter what other strongholds he claimed. But 'palace' is a misleading term; Kincora was actually a very large stone and timber fort, containing a great hall and royal apartments among its principal rooms. It stood amid the numerous smaller offices necessary for supporting the entourage of a great king. The entire compound, surrounded by a high timber palisade, was capable of garrisoning hundreds of warriors in addition to housing Brian's growing family and entertaining an endless procession of guests.

Although Brian would make many alterations in Kincora over the years, seeking to improve it as his own stature grew, one of its fittings was unvarying. Tradition dictated that a royal candle of enormous size with a great bushy wick must always be kept burning at night in the presence of a king. A special iron candle holder as straight as a spear was designed for this purpose. The young man whose job was to light the king-candle every night and extinguish it with the coming of dawn was an honoured member of the royal entourage. He was the king's personal attendant, and at all times wore a bag belted to his waist containing flints and a steel for striking fire.

Tradition also required that a king have a poet. Brian's was a man called Mac Liag, for whom Brian built a home on a little island in nearby Lough Derg. The island is still there. With its memories.

Brian had never been outside of Ireland. At the time he built Kincora he had not even seen the stronghold of the current Árd Rí, so he was free to build his residence limited only by the bounds of his imagination. The annalists claim that Brian personally designed two separate passages connecting the banqueting hall with the kitchens, one passage to be used by servants carrying the food in, and the other for removing the empty serving dishes. The exact seating arrangements in the banqueting hall were carefully drawn on a large chart to make sure there were no lapses in protocol. Kings and princes, poets and judges each had their special place of honour.

By this period there is no further mention of Mor, or even of Achra, in the annals, although the children they had borne to Brian were with him at Kincora. Achra's son Domnall would die there of an illness in 1009 or 1010, but Mor's Murrough would be with Brian for the rest of his life. All that Brian Boru knew or achieved would be Murrough's inheritance.

Amongst the traditions Brian chose to overthrow was that of tanistry, by which a king's successor was elected from amongst suitable members of the royal family. Brian Boru left nothing to chance. He was determined that Murrough would be his successor, heir not only to his power but to his every thought and idea. The best of Brian would go into the son who was most like him. As a grown man, Murrough may have resented his father's continuing efforts to educate him, but it was necessary. Someday he would be grateful.

Kincora is long gone but Béal Boru is still there, defying time. The remains of the ancient ringfort are two kilometres north of the present village of Killaloe. One may still observe sections of stone wall smothered in ivy, fittingly crowned by trees. In Brian's time Béal Boru was the location of a major ford on the Shannon, Ireland's largest river, which divided east from west. Roughly translated, Béal Boru means 'The Mouth (or Gateway) of the Cattle Tribute'. A sizeable percentage of the cattle travelling longitudinally across Ireland would cross the river at this point. It would be hard to overestimate the ford's importance to a cattle-based economy. Control of the ford from their nearby stronghold probably gave Brian's Dalcassian ancestors their original power.

If it is possible to deduce a man's character from his actions, by now we have an idea of Brian Boru. But what of his opposite number, his sometime ally and frequent opponent, Malachy Mór? Malachy had been born in 948, seven years after Brian, with every expectation of a rich and satisfying life. His parents were of the princely class and he had the unqualified support of the powerful Uí Néill. All he had to do was behave as a high king should, following traditions laid down for centuries.

Like Brian, Malachy Mór kept a scribe at his elbow throughout his career, commemorating his victories and praising his hospitality. We have only one surviving comment from Malachy about the Battle of Clontarf: the most horrific eyewitness account of all comes from his scribe.

Most of Malachy's contemporaries, if they were not engaged in battle with him, liked the man. The annalists portray him as a generous, gregarious individual, a real 'man's man', who was well suited for the traditional niche he held in life. He was simple in the way that strong men were simple in those times. He lacked the labyrinthine turns of mind of a Brian Boru.

Undoubtedly he was brave, however, and able to uphold the demands of his kingship. When provincial kings tested their power against him he always rose to the challenge. Connacht and Leinster were proving particularly troublesome, with their tribes invading other provinces, raiding cattle and generally disregarding the law. For almost fifteen years both Malachy in Meath and Brian Boru in Munster would be engaged in sporadic warfare with belligerent tribes who refused to accept their individual authority. The ongoing divisions within Ireland made stable governance almost impossible.

Brian won such battles more often than Malachy Mór. In 988 Brian sailed his fleet up the Shannon and delivered a stinging defeat to an army of recalcitrant Connachtmen at Lough Ree. It was probably shortly after this that he married Duvcholly. Thereafter the province of Connacht was less hostile, at least to him.

Alas for Malachy Mór, he did not have an asset like Duvcholly. Soon after marrying Gormlaith of Leinster he realised he had stepped into a hornet's nest. Her temper was sudden and explosive; her moods violent and unpredictable. Meanwhile, Gormlaith made discoveries of her own. A virile warrior king in his middle years could not be bullied like doddering old Olaf Cuaran, nor could he be manipulated like her callow son, Sitric. Gormlaith was not content with the placid role in life the Árd Rí assigned to her, so she began casting about for a way to amuse herself. The Árd Rí was away from home for long periods at a time. And Dublin was only a few days' journey in good weather.

In 989 Malachy Mór learned of a rebellion simmering in Dublin as the result of a conspiracy between some of the Leinstermen and the Danes. Malachy promptly laid siege to the city. Sitric Silkbeard surrendered without putting up too much struggle, and promised to pay an ounce of gold for every garden in Dublin. Perhaps it was this which subsequently inspired Sitric to strike some of the earliest coins produced in Ireland. They had the profile of Gormlaith's son on them.

While Sitric in Dublin nursed his hurt pride, perhaps with his mother at his elbow, Malachy Mór and Brian

Boru kept encountering one another on the battle-field. The warriors of Leinster and the Danes of Dublin observed from afar, hoping that the two men would wear each other down and leave an opening for a new power in the land.

When Maelmora, Gormlaith's brother, was elected king of Leinster, Sitric at once made a formal offer of the resources of his own kingdom to Maelmora, forgetting his earlier submission to Malachy Mór. One might sense Gormlaith's fine hand in this. Her second marriage had not made her happy – if anything could. The annals do not record whether it was Malachy or Brian who suggested that the two of them combine their forces against Leinster and the Danes, but it may have been Tara that sent an emissary to Kincora. When his back was to the wall, Malachy usually did the prudent thing. An alliance with the 'Lion of Munster' was definitely the prudent thing.

For once, the interests of the two kings were converging, with a common enemy in Leinster. In 999 Brian Boru marched northwards to combine his army with that of Malachy Mór. Maelmora led his forces out to do battle with the two kings, accompanied by a large contingent from Dublin, warriors sworn to his nephew, Sitric Silkbeard. They met at a place called Glenmama, near Saggart in County Dublin. The battle was savage, with heavy casualties on both sides. A large number of Leinstermen died while attempting to escape. At Brian's order they were surrounded and driven into a flooded ford on the Liffey like so many cattle, then slaughtered on the bank as they tried to get out. Among the slain was Harald, a son of Olaf Cuaran, which made him a half-brother to Sitric Silkbeard.

When it was obvious the tide of battle had turned against him, Maelmora, fearing capture, hid amongst the darkly funereal branches of a yew tree. There he was discovered by Brian's son, Murrough. Murrough dragged the humiliated king of Leinster from his perch in the tree while the warriors laughed and made rude remarks. In an act of generosity worthy of his father, Murrough spared Maelmora's life – an act he would live to regret.

On the following day, Malachy and Brian marched into Dublin and sacked the prosperous port city. The air was black with the smoke of burning shops and warehouses. Carts were piled high with valuables to be sent back to Dun na Sciath and Kincora. When Sitric offered grudging submission to both kings, his offer was accepted. At Brian's behest the defeated Dubliners were allowed to return to their homes. Maelmora was given permission to take his surviving warriors back to Naas – although they had to leave their weapons behind.

We do not know if Gormlaith was in Dublin visiting Sitric when Malachy and Brian arrived with their armies. But she well may have been; she may have seen her husband beside Brian Boru. Malachy was the Árd Rí, but Brian Boru, according to the annalists of the day, was splendid. Their overwhelming victory over the Leinstermen and their Danish allies was dramatic proof that Irishmen united could accomplish what Irishmen divided could not. Unfortunately it was a lesson that would not outlive them.

Brian remained encamped in Dublin from Christmas through most of February. This gave him an opportunity to familiarise himself with the territory. It was a commander's habit of reconnaissance which must have been second nature to him by this time. He also would have observed the sea, the darkly turbulent sea that lapped the city walls on the east and dominated the lives and fortunes of its inhabitants.

Meanwhile Malachy Mór had returned to Dun na Sciath to celebrate. At Glenmama he had observed some of the clever tactics of Brian Boru. The victory had not been his alone and he knew it, but any victory was worth celebrating. He also summoned the brehons to witness that he was setting aside – the Irish term for divorce – his wife, the princess Gormlaith. This was only a small victory for Malachy, but one he obviously felt was necessary.

As the sun set on the last day of February, Brian returned to Kincora. He could never stay away for long. He needed the fragrant silence of the forested hills at his back, needed the gleaming sweep of the Shannon at his feet. By now he could see, quite clearly, the road fate had laid out for him. He knew his own strength and the strengths and weaknesses of the Árd Rí. There could be no going back, all the chessmen were in place. It was time for the next move on the board.

To the astonishment of many, Brian arranged a marriage between his daughter, Emer, and Sitric Silkbeard, thus acknowledging his former opponent as a worthy son-in-law. But there was another surprise in store. At about the same time Brian married Sitric's mother, Gormlaith, the former wife of two kings. The ultimate trophy.

This latest marriage of Brian's may not have taken place with religious solemnities; there is simply no record one way or the other. But it served its purpose. If she was a secondary wife as allowed under Brehon law, she was nevertheless in a position of prestige. Mindful of Brian's unparalleled rise to power and his generosity to the Church, the clergy kept silent about any misgivings.

Throughout his career he was always careful to keep the Church on his side.

Here we are allowed a brief glimpse into the private life of Malachy Mór. Imagine how very hard he laughed, and how very much he drank at the banquet table, when he learned that his erstwhile rival had saddled himself with a liability like Gormlaith.

There has been some question as to the order in which Gormlaith married her men, but a poem composed shortly after her death contains a clue:

Gormlaith took three leaps,
which a woman shall never take again
A leap at Ath-cliath [Dublin], a leap at Teamhair [Tara],
A leap at Caiseal [Cashel] of the goblets over all.

This would indicate that she married Olaf Cuaran first, followed by Malachy Mór, and finally Brian, whose royal seat was Cashel, although he ruled from Kincora. Duvcholly was probably still alive when Brian brought his new wife home to the palace beside the Shannon. Whether or not Duvcholly had children by Brian we do not know. But although she was middle-aged herself by this time, Gormlaith soon conceived and bore Brian a son. They called him Donough.

The alliance of Brian and Malachy which had proved

successful at Glenmama was a fragile one. Since that victory there had been frequent skirmishes between Brian's warriors and those of the high king. The brief truce which had been to their mutual advantage could not last. Two powerful kings could not share one small island.

In the autumn of 1002 Brian Boru marched an army to Dun na Sciath, demanding that Malachy Mór give battle to him there or submit the high kingship. Malachy replied by asking for a month to gather his forces. Brian agreed. Malachy made his best effort but could not collect enough men willing to fight Brian Boru. At the end of the allotted time the Árd Rí, accompanied only by his personal bodyguards, went to Brian's camp. There he submitted without imposing any conditions. His confidence in the Dalcassian's sense of honour was not misplaced. Brian treated Malachy with respect and even returned to him the fine horses he had offered in tribute.

Malachy's contemporaries also respected him. The annalists praised him in the fulsome language of the time, and his partisans resented his treatment at the hands of the upstart Dalcassian. Yet once he died he was all but forgotten, like his predecessors. If it were not for Brian Boru, Malachy's name would be unknown today. Yet his was an unusual career. He became Árd Rí in 980 and again in 1015, the only man in the history of Ireland to bear that title twice. As high kings go, he was as good as most and better than some. Unfortunately for Malachy Mór, by the time he died in 1022 he had lived most of his life in the shadow of a larger man.

By making himself Árd Rí, Brian had challenged and effectively overthrown the ancient rule of the kingly houses of Tara and Aileach. He almost might be described as a 'land leaper' himself; he certainly was reviled in some quarters as a usurper. Yet in his lifetime he would accomplish more for the whole of Ireland than the Uí Néill kings had done in centuries.

Although they would not face him in battle, the princes of the north continued to resent Brian, sullenly refusing to acknowledge his authority – until 1004. While conducting a royal circuit of Ireland that year he visited Armagh, St Patrick's holy city, and confirmed the primacy of the city with an entry made in the *Book of Armagh*. In one final, irrefutable gesture, the entry was signed by his secretary and close friend: 'This I have written, namely, Maolsuthain ua Cearbhaill, in the presence of Brian, Imperator Scotorum' – Emperor of the Irish. Brian also left twenty ounces of pure gold, which was an immense sum, on the high altar of the cathedral.

It would be unfair to Brian to interpret this extravagant gesture as merely a cynical bribe. This was the man who had been repairing and rebuilding churches and monasteries for years. He was well aware that St Patrick's holy cathedral had repeatedly suffered from raids, and in 996 had been nearly destroyed by a lightning strike that damaged its roof beyond repair. Twenty ounces of gold would buy a lot of slate and pay for the finest workmanship.

There was no further overt resistance to Brian from the northern Uí Néill. Although they never openly acknowledged him as Árd Rí, Brian took their submission as a given. As far as he was concerned the entire island was his to protect. He willed his body to Armagh and his soul to God. In 1014 Armagh would return the favour by giving Brian Boru the most magnificent funeral ever seen in Ireland.

During his reign as high king Brian continued with his programme of construction, ignoring provincial boundaries and requesting no permissions from provincial kings. Because he realised that a strong permanent force would be necessary to secure the island from any further invasion, Brian continued to demand discipline from his army. He controversially insisted that the warriors of the Gael welcome Norse and Dane into their ranks. The Vikings had been in Ireland for generations by now, he argued, and their children and grandchildren knew no other home. They should be willing to fight for it. At the Battle of Clontarf, Brian's Vikings would be amongst his best fighters.

Although he himself would never leave Ireland, apparently Brian thought in terms of creating a dynasty with a longer reach. He had begun by marrying his daughter Sabia to Cian, which had given the Dalcassians a broader base in the south. While still king of Munster, Brian arranged for his daughter Blanaid to wed Malcolm, prince of Alba – the ancient name for Scotland. There was a strange symmetry to this marriage. The highlands where Malcolm was born had been settled in the sixth century by the Dal Riada tribe from the north of Ireland, the 'Scoti', hence the name of Scot Land. In 1005 Brian's son-in-law was crowned Malcolm II, king of Scotland.

Two years later, one of Blanaid and Malcolm's daughters married Sigurd the Stout, earl of Orkney. After the Battle of Clontarf their son Thorfinn was raised by his grandfather, Malcolm II. In 1040 Thorfinn took up arms against his cousin Duncan, who had succeeded Malcolm as king of the Scots. Duncan was defeated at the Battle of Torfness, and afterward was murdered by another cousin who aspired to the kingship, Macbeth – whose grandmother was the daughter of Brian Boru. Macbeth and Thorfinn ruled Scotland between them until both died in 1057.

When Brian married his daughter Emer to Sitric Silk-beard, king of the Dublin Danes, he must have hoped to establish a more amicable relationship between Gael and foreigner. It might have been possible if human nature had been different. In the final analysis Brian was, more than anything else, a tribal chieftain working for the benefit of his tribe and clan. He was trying to give them something of lasting value. And he very nearly succeeded.

Duvcholly died in 1009, leaving Gormlaith as the only queen at Kincora. Brian's other wives have disappeared from history, having taken no active part in events. But Gormlaith was active enough to make up for them all. Her tempestuous nature caused constant problems at Kincora, where she was greatly resented by the other women in the king's large entourage. Fortunately for them, Gormlaith's tenure was drawing towards its close, though there was a final spectacular performance before she left the stage. And even after her death in 1030, something of her would remain in the fray ...

There would also be one more dynastic marriage, although Brian would not live to see it. Years after the Battle of Clontarf, Donough, Gormlaith's son by Brian Boru, married Driella, the youngest daughter of God-wine, earl of Kent. Godwine's other daughter, Edytha, was married to King Edward the Confessor. Their brother by their Danish mother, Gytha, was Harold Godwine, who would become the last of the Saxon kings of England.

Through Brian Boru's children and grandchildren his blood entered the royal bloodlines of Europe, where it still appears in family trees today.

• • • • • • •

CHAPTER FIVE

A Spark in Dry Tinder

There are almost as many ways to start wars as there are men to fight them, but the sparks that ignited the Battle of Clontarf may have been struck over a chess board. However, it all began with cows. A lot of cows.

Over the centuries the tributes demanded by Irish kings had caused endless trouble, which usually centred on the number of cattle involved. The size of a man's herd determined his status within the tribe. An overwhelming percentage of the cattle population consisted of cows, the bovine male being considered inferior – there are no beef-eating heroes in Irish literature; wild boar was the champion's protein of choice. Bulls were maintained only for breeding, bull calves were killed for their leather, and bullocks were unheard-of. Sheep were raised for wool and pigs for meat, but the cow was the measure of everything: the unit of value, the primary medium of exchange. Although the life of the community revolved around cows, only women were allowed to milk them. Milk and its products formed a large part of the daily diet. The cow was almost a member of society, and hers was an essential role in calculating tributes.

The Book of Rights spelt out in precise detail the size of every tribute, so no argument would be possible. But this was Ireland. Argument was always possible.

During his reign as Árd Rí, Brian gave Ireland a decade of relative peace. There were occasions which demanded a show of strength, as when in 1006 he had to march into Ulster and demand hostages in order to put down a tribal rebellion. But the poets were able to relate with pride:

From Torach to pleasant Cliodlinna
And robed in all her finery,
In the time of Brian, of high side and fearless,
A lone woman made the circuit of Erin
And no man accosted her.

1010 was a bad year for Brian. Domnall, the younger of his two sons by Achra, died of an illness at Kincora. Shortly afterwards Brian received word that his last living brother, Marcan, who had risen through the ranks of the clergy to become abbot of Emly and chief of the clergy of Munster, had also died.

Brian and death were old acquaintances. But he was sixty-nine and this was bringing it very close to home, reminding him of his own mortality at a time when such things begin to weigh on a man. He must have felt the need to consolidate his holdings.

At a time lost in antiquity a huge tribute had been demanded of a king of Leinster by a king of Connacht who defeated him in battle. Known as the Boru Tribute, or 'cattle tax', this originally consisted of slaves, coverlets, cauldrons, hogs ... and cows. Thousands of cows. On their way to the west from Leinster an immense herd was driven across the Shannon at the ford which became known as Béal Boru – 'The Gateway of the Cattle Tribute'. The Boru Tribute continued to be paid in this way for generations, until eventually the tribute was forgiven or forgotten.

In 1012, and without warning, Brian reintroduced the hated Boru Tribute upon Leinster and its current king, Maelmora. According to the Book of Rights, the only tribute Leinster specifically owed to the Árd Rí was 'the venison of Naas'. As king of Munster, Brian was due 'the privilege of burning north Leinster.' But Brian was the high king now, and unwilling to settle for tokens.

He wanted a full scale submission from Maelmora, one which the king of Leinster could not refute without sacrificing his honour. To this end Brian demanded great herds of cattle and swine, woollen mantles, silver chains, copper cauldrons, bronze pails, and more besides.

Maelmora was incandescent with rage. He should not have been surprised. The ancient conflict between Munster and Leinster had never really ended. In spite of Brian's efforts to establish peace, warriors from Leinster had continued to make frequent incursions into the rest of Leth Moga and Maelmora had made no effort to discourage their behaviour. In fact he encouraged it. He was happy to have the cattle they stole fattening on his grass.

Maelmora's pride and arrogance had been sorely tested by having a Munster man claim authority over him. Gormlaith's marriage to the Árd Rí had not encouraged her belligerent brother to mend his ways. The marriage itself was a disaster, as everyone knew. For Maelmora this was just another reason to hold a grudge against Brian Boru. He had rejoiced in every little cut his men took at Brian's authority.

Reimposing the Boru Tribute brought the rivalry between the two men to a whole new level. Sourly, the king of Leinster considered his options. They were very few. He knew Brian of old, and was sure the Árd Rí would enforce his demand to the letter. In fact, within days of being informed of the reintroduction of the Boru Tribute, Maelmora learned that Brian's son, Murrough, had led an army into one of Leinster's tributary kingdoms, Ossory. They were sweeping across the land, seizing spoils and taking prisoners.

It was an open invitation to war – a war Maelmora was unprepared to fight against the full power of the high king. But what else could he do? If he sat on his hands and did nothing his people would turn against him. The Gael were a warrior race. A leader who failed to answer the challenge to battle would soon be overthrown. Or worse.

At Naas the king of Leinster paced through his fort, swore at his women and kicked his hounds.

Once again, Brian did the unexpected. While Maelmora was struggling to find a solution to his problem, a messenger brought a graciously worded request from Kincora. Would it be possible for the king of Leinster to supply the Árd Rí with three tall masts for his fleet on the Shannon? The Árd Rí would be most grateful. The implication was obvious. By gifting Brian Boru with three of the mightiest oaks in Leinster, Maelmora might hope to escape further punishment.

The astonished Maelmora hastened to comply. His fort

was thrown into chaos as he called for his finest apparel and jewels, collected whatever baubles he could find to offer as further diplomatic gifts, and sent gangs of foresters to locate and cut down the tallest oaks in the province. He also demanded a company of strong men from the three foremost Leinster clans. Each clan would be responsible for carrying one mast to Kincora. Maelmora's own clan, of course, would carry the largest. The entire procession would make a fine display.

Crowds gathered outside Naas to watch the king and his party set out. It was a festive occasion. Women waved, children cheered, and barking dogs got in the way. The journey took almost a week, with Maelmora demanding his men trot at top speed every step of the way. By the time they reached the east bank of the Shannon everyone was tired and out of sorts. Maelmora, however, insisted he felt as strong as ever. Before they stepped onto the bridge which Brian had built to span the river above the ford, Maelmora ostentatiously put his own shoulder to the largest mast. The rough timber tore a heavy silver ornament from his tunic, a royal gift from Brian Boru in an earlier time.

Maelmora tucked the ornament into the gilded bag of personal valuables that he carried around his waist, and completed his journey.

At Kincora the king of Leinster was greeted by Brian himself with elaborate courtesy. There was the customary exchange of gifts. Maelmora's entourage was directed to their quarters while the two kings shared goblets of red wine and chewed on honeycomb in the great hall. They discussed the weather, the condition of the roads, the length and weight of the timber masts. No mention was made of the Boru Tribute. Nor of Gormlaith, who did not appear at the welcoming ceremony. Brian assured Maelmora that his sister would be joining them for a celebratory banquet that evening. Meanwhile Maelmora was to enjoy all the hospitality the palace could offer, which was considerable. Brian had ordered an exceptionally lavish display put on for the king of Leinster.

Brian's generosity to a defeated foe was legendary. Acting through Murrough, Brian had punished enough of Leinster to satisfy himself. He then had forced its king to an act of submission, and was now willing to forgive if not forget, provided Maelmora behaved himself in future. Turning enemies into friends, or at least allies, was one of Brian's many tactics. It could be of advantage to both sides.

What followed became part of Irish folklore. The incident, which has several versions, may or may not have happened at all, but given the natures of the people involved there may well be a germ of truth in the story.

Maelmora was basically a simple man who did not recognise the occasion for what it was. He was still spoiling for a fight. With set face and gritted teeth he endured the formalities being pressed upon him. He may even have thought Brian was mocking him. He dared not attack the Árd Rí in his own stronghold, with armed guards at every doorway, but there was someone on whom Maelmorda could vent his simmering anger. As soon as Gormlaith appeared, her brother took the silver ornament from his bag and handed it to her, demanding that she sew it back on. Like a servant. She who had married three kings!

Eyes flashing, hair tossing, face white with fury, Gormlaith hurled the ornament into the fire. She roundly cursed her brother, condemning him for having accepted Brian's 'bribe' in the first place. She assailed the king of Leinster with the most cruel insults from their shared childhood, and even called him the high king's lap dog.

Brian was dismayed. His attempt to establish amity with the king of Leinster was being torn to shreds. Over the years the Árd Rí had learned to control his temper, but this time Gormlaith had gone too far. With a grim face, Brian led her from the great hall to the privacy of their own chambers. There, following what must have been a protracted and monumental quarrel, he told Gormlaith he was going to set her aside.

For a woman of her temperament the insult was beyond bearing. Gormlaith demanded the best horse in the king's stable – as a noblewoman she was entitled to ride – and prepared to depart that same afternoon for Dublin. Sitric Silkbeard would give his mother the respect she deserved!

Gormlaith and the attendants who accompanied her on her journey would be following a road made safe for female travellers by Brian Boru.

In the clear light of a new morning Brian might have regretted his decision to divorce her. He, who could take the long view and foresee consequences, might even have sent for Gormlaith to come back to him. But there was no time. Before the day was over something far worse had happened.

While Gormlaith and Brian were preoccupied with their quarrel, Murrough had returned to Kincora sooner than expected. He and Maelmora were badly startled to encounter one another in the hall. With an effort at princely dignity, the two men managed to limit their reactions to a curt nod and an icy stare. Murrough went to the apartments set aside for him, washed himself and put on fresh clothing. He then returned to the great hall and engaged Conaing, Brian's nephew, in a game of chess. Although it was a ploy to pass the time until Brian joined them, both men took the match seriously. Chess was always taken seriously. Spectators gathered to watch the match.

Although it was not yet midday the great hall of Kincora was brilliantly lit, ablaze with firelight as well as the flickering flames of hundreds of beeswax candles. Brian liked to keep the shadows at a distance. Scented rushes were piled calf-deep on the flagged floor, adding their perfume to the fragrance of pine cones burning on the hearth. Scores of the high king's guests, numerous courtiers and members of his own extended family eddied about the hall, talking, laughing, exchanging the gossip of the day. Anticipating the banquet to come. At one end of the long room a harper played softly, with his eyes closed and his head bent over his instrument. Kincora was dreaming, waiting for Brian Boru to bring it awake.

With a heavy silver cup in his hand, Maelmora sauntered over to join the spectators around the chess table. The king of Leinster drained his cup and set it down, then leaned against the nearest carved and painted oak pillar and folded his arms across his chest. A sneer of contempt was hidden by his beard. After a few minutes he called attention to a possible move Murrough had overlooked. Brian's son heard the remark but was not aware who had spoken. He took Maelmora's suggestion. At his opponent's very next move, Murrough realised the move had cost him the game. Whirling around on his stool, he saw the king of Leinster grinning at him.

'That was the sort of advice you gave the Danes at Glenmama!' Murrough burst out.

Maelmora replied with equal rancour. 'The next time I give them advice they won't be defeated.'

Both men were on their feet now, fists clenched. Murrough shouted at the Leinsterman, 'Then, you coward, you had best tell them to have a yew tree ready for you to hide in!'

Or so the story goes. Now, no Irishman called another a coward with impunity. Knowing he dare not kill Murrough where he stood, the enraged king of Leinster stormed out of the hall. He and his followers left Kincora without waiting to bid Brian farewell. In a short time they were on their way to Naas.

When the Árd Rí returned to the great hall his people crowded around him, elbowing one another aside in their eagerness to relate the dramatic incident. From the moment he glimpsed Murrough's face, however, Brian knew all he needed to know. He ordered a messenger to hurry after the king of Leinster and invite him – with profuse apologies – to return to Kincora, so that matters between the two kings could be peacefully resolved.

Maelmora was in no mood to be pacified. When Brian's messenger caught up with the Leinstermen, Maelmora himself beat the hapless man to death with a horse-rod made of yew wood and left him on the side of the road with his brains spilling out of his skull. By the time his body was found it was too late for anyone to stop what had been put in motion.

Maelmora summoned the heads of the Leinster tribes to an assembly at Naas. There he described how he and the entire province had been mistreated by the so-called high king. The usurper from Thomond must be destroyed! Nothing else would satisfy the honour of Leinster.

Even in the grip of rage, Maelmora knew he could not defeat Brian Boru without help. He sent envoys to seek aid from every king and chieftain in the land, promising battlefield glory. Success attracts begrudgers and Brian's success was almost incomprehensible to less gifted men; although his firm allies remained loyal to him, petty kings whose allegiance to the Árd Rí was less than certain began to waiver. Wondering if there was something in this for them.

But when Maelmora's request reached the princes of

the Uí Néill, Malachy Mór actually refused to side with the king of Leinster against the man who had taken his throne.

In Dublin, Gormlaith ranted about the abuse she had suffered at Brian's hands. Sitric Silkbeard repudiated his father-in-law and revoked any submission to him. The Danes of Dublin were told to prepare for battle, one more time. Sitric was still young, but he was no fool. Like Maelmora he was aware that Brian Boru would be hard to defeat if he was fully roused. This time they must hand the old man a defeat from which he could never recover. Without Brian Boru, Ireland would be ripe for conquest. The potential for plunder would be immense. What an opportunity it would be for the right men! Sitric became very busy indeed.

Bad news travels faster than good news. Throughout the five provinces it soon became known that a revolt against Brian Boru was in the making.

Usually so decisive, Brian had yet to act. The abrupt unravelling of the plans he had implemented over so many years seems to have unsettled the ageing high king. His sons stepped into the breach. Murrough, in particular, was very busy from 1010 to 1012, perhaps to help put the death of his brother, Domnall, out of his mind. Again and again he led the Dalcassians and their allies against dissident chieftains. Once one was put down, another sprang up. Rogue bands infiltrated Louth and even royal Meath, fomenting rebellion. Murrough complained to his father, 'They are not content to be content!'

Maelmora asked the king of Aileach, a prince of the Uí Néill and thus one of Malachy's own kinsmen, to attack Meath and intimidate Malachy's followers to such an extent that Brian Boru would get no help from that province. An expeditionary force composed of warriors from what is now Cavan, Leitrim and Longford marched on Malachy's fortress, Dun na Sciath. The invaders put the fort to the torch and ravaged the surrounding territory. One of Malachy's sons was slain as he fought to defend his clan's hereditary stronghold.

In an attempt to show himself as Brian's staunch ally – and thus discourage Aileach from making any further attacks on him – Malachy led an army to battle the combined forces of Sitric and his uncle Maelmora outside of Dublin. He paid a high price for this political move. Malachy's troops were soundly defeated and another of his sons was killed in the fighting.

A deeply disheartened Malachy Mór finally appealed to Brian Boru for help. It must have been hard for the former high king to swallow his pride, but Brian rewarded him with an instant and positive response. The Árd Rí's army, reinforced by a contingent from Connacht and another from the Northmen of Waterford, marched into Leinster, burned Naas and thoroughly routed Maelmora's men. Brian himself stayed in the province for three months while his combined army plundered southern Leinster. The victors then marched on to Dublin and blockaded the city for another three months.

But the tactics of siege and blockade were not strong points with the Gael. They were too eager for action, too ready to fight. Plus the weather was against them. The ground froze and the game fled; the farmers in the area were hostile and determined to hang onto whatever resources they had. It became increasingly difficult for the army to live off the land. As Christmas approached, their supplies dwindled until Brian had to face the possibility of a mutiny in the New Year. Reluctantly, he gave the order to return to Kincora. There he could rest and gather his energies, and prepare for the future. After an indecisive campaign he badly needed a brilliant success to maintain his supremacy. He was no longer a young man. He knew that one more battle would probably be his last.

Just one more great victory to cement all he had accomplished.

Then he could live out his days beside the Shannon,

below Craglea, in the palace he loved, where every room, every passageway and outbuilding was of his own design. He could see it so clearly. He would gather his entire family around him. Murrough and Flann and Conor and Tadhg and their wives and children, nieces and nephews and cousins. All together under one broad roof. His clan. They would eat at his table and sit by his fire, safe in the knowledge that their future was as secure as Brian Boru could make it.

Sitric Silkbeard, many years younger than Brian and born with a belligerent disposition, wanted a great victory too. Brian's ignominious retreat to Kincora – that was how Sitric saw it – told him the old man was used up and ready for the killing stroke. To destroy the Irish Árd Rí would enhance Sitric's reputation beyond anything his ancestors had done. Of almost equal importance, it would please his mother, possibly even put a stop to her increasingly hysterical tirades.

Gormlaith seemed intent on making her son's homelife a hell on earth. Night and day she spewed out her hatred for the man who had been the third king to reject her. The third king who did not want her! To Gormlaith, Brian must have represented all the cruelty and injustice in the world.

Sitric's mother's loathing for Brian Boru was counterbalanced by his wife's oft-expressed admiration for her father, that same Brian Boru. Marrying Sitric had not made Emer a Viking woman; she would remain Brian's daughter and a proud Dalcassian all her life. She boasted of her lineage at every opportunity and denigrated Gormlaith's Leinster blood. The two women were frequently at one another's throats while Sitric was caught in the middle. A king should not have to live like that! Brian Boru must finally cease to be a blight on Sitric's life.

Sitric Silkbeard found a way.

CHAPTER SIX

THE NORTHERN
CONSPIRACY

In the dead of winter, when Scapa Flow was like a sheet of beaten lead and his men were yawning with boredom, the earl of Orkney was pleasantly surprised to receive a royal deputation from Ireland. Three longships flying Danish banners arrived with the setting sun over their shoulders. The commander of the little fleet was no less than Sitric Silkbeard. Beneath a heavy cloak he was dressed in his most impressive royal regalia. Around his neck was a massive gold collar. His brown hair was divided into neat plaits, as was his beard. Before setting foot on land he fixed a gold circlet securely on his brow.

Sigurd the Stout hastened to give the king of Dublin

a royal welcome. Sheep and goats who had been quietly grazing on the sparse grass were snatched up, their throats cut, and their bodies skewered over open firepits while they were still twitching. The earl's servitors scoured the settlement that had grown up around his stronghold, demanding the best food and drink for his visitors. Small stone ovens were emptied of cooling bread while the women of the house wailed at their loss and complained that their children would be left starving. Nets full of freshly caught fish were seized from angry fishermen at water's edge and carried on the run to the earl's kitchens.

While slaves showed Sitric and his party to the thatched guesting house and urged them to rest themselves after their journey, frantic activity was taking place elsewhere. Large vats of beer and ale were being dragged into Sigurd's great hall, which resembled the overturned body of a massive boat. When the vats were opened their yeasty fragrance filled the room.

That evening an extravagant feast was served by torchlight. Shadows danced beneath the curved ceiling. In honour of his guests Sigurd even allowed his womenfolk to attend, though of course they did not eat with the men. The party lasted late into the night and well into the next day. When little was left but gnawed bones and breadcrumbs – and drunken men sprawling on the floor of the hall – Sigurd settled himself to hear what his guest had to say. He expected the ruler of Dublin had come in person to offer him a new and beneficial trade proposal.

Instead, Sitric said he was organising a rebellion in cooperation with his uncle, the king of Leinster. Their purpose was to overthrow the Irish high king, Brian Boru. For this bold move, Sitric was recruiting allies amongst the Vikings of the northern isles.

Now Sigurd really was surprised. Even in the Orkneys, Brian's name and career were familiar. Norse longships carried information across the sea much more quickly than news of events could travel over land. Brian Boru had long been a hero figure to the Scandinavians, who celebrated an exceptional warrior no matter what his race. As late as the thirteenth century the prolific Icelandic writer, Snorre Sturlasson, would refer to Clontarf simply as 'the Brian battle', indicating that Brian Boru was still so well known that no further explanation was necessary.

Sigurd the Stout knew that Ireland was politically fragmented and socially unstable. He also believed the Gael suffered from a sort of madness that made them willing to fight to the death in order to hold onto treacherous bogs and impenetrable forests. For these reasons, any attempt to conquer the entire island would involve battling one disparate tribe after another, year after year, until the invader's men were used up and the prize was as distant as ever, which was why no northern warlord had tried it in the past. Yet under the Dalcassian Árd Rí, there was said to be unity between some of the most bellicose chieftains. There were also rumours of new roads being cut through forests and bogs being drained to create arable farmland.

Ireland had begun to look like a land worth conquering.

The earl of Orkney leaned forward and propped his elbows on his knees, listening intently to what Sitric had to say. This was more than a trade proposal; it could be an opportunity of almost unlimited scope. But getting involved would have its dangers. Sigurd was a wily man who had not achieved his place in life by taking foolish risks. If he was going to lend his support to this plan he would have to have guarantees, he told Sitric. A promise of unlimited plunder, perhaps? And slaves?

Sitric smiled. He replied that he was prepared to make a most generous offer, one the other man surely could not turn down. Plunder and slaves, of course – that went without saying. But if the earl of Orkney would bring an army of Vikings to fight on the rebels' behalf, his reward would be nothing less than the kingdom of Ireland itself.

Sigurd stroked his lower lip. He cleared his throat. After

a suitable interval he inquired – as if the answer were of little concern – how Sitric could make such an offer. Would it include the city of Dublin? Was young Silk-beard offering to give up his own kingship? Or, for that matter, would the king of Leinster surrender his?

Sitric had expected this and was prepared. He and Maelmora would retain their titles, he said smoothly, but Sigurd the Stout would be their overlord. They would cede to him ownership of the prosperous trading ports along the east coast and the grazing of all of Leinster. In effect, the earl of Orkney would hold the eastern half of Ireland. From such a position and freed of Brian Boru's interference, he could easily extend his control to the entire island.

Still Sigurd hesitated. It was a spectacular offer; almost too spectacular; it smacked of desperation. He guessed there was something Sitric was holding back, a last-ditch bribe he hoped would clinch the deal.

There was. By all evidence, Sitric Silkbeard had a devious mind. Before travelling to the Orkneys he had weighed up what he had to offer and found it lacking. He had decided on one final temptation to throw into the pot: his mother.

If Brian Boru had achieved near-legendary status, his third wife had not done so badly herself. Sitric knew perfectly well that Gormlaith was no longer the beauty she once had been. At best she was an old woman who still possessed the fine bones and queenly stature of her youth. She also was vain and greedy and had a viper's tongue. Yet three separate, and prestigious, kings had chosen her as wife. Three kings! Surely no other woman would ever come close to that achievement again. A woman as unique as Gormlaith would be a prize beyond valuing.

And if she was claimed by Sigurd the Stout, her son would be rid of her forever.

Of course, there was every possibility that the earl of Orkney might die in battle and not take Gormlaith after all. Sitric Silkbeard had a contingency plan for this, which he did not divulge to his host. In a game of chess no move was announced in advance.

Sigurd the Stout listened with incredulity as he was offered Gormlaith's hand in marriage. This was something he had never anticipated. He had plenty of women at his disposal, including a child bride, but nothing like the woman the Norse sagas already were referring to as Kormlada. She was more splendid than the rising sun! Or so they said.

He leaned forward, unaware that his mouth had fallen open, while Sitric went into rapturous detail about his mother's ageless beauty. Her ankle-length hair, her full bosom. Not to mention her kindly disposition and her personal fortune. All the earl of Orkney had to do was kill the Irish high king and Gormlaith would be his, together with the kingdom of Ireland. Once Brian Boru was gone, Sitric insisted, both would fall into Sigurd's lap like ripe fruit. It was more than mere flesh and blood could resist.

Sigurd agreed to the proposal, then ordered a feast of gargantuan proportions prepared in celebration.

Throughout the rest of that day and the day following, the two men discussed plans for the invasion of Ireland. Earl Sigurd boasted that he could mobilise the entire fleet of the Western Isles and also draw additional auxiliaries from the Scandinavian mainland. Tens of thousands, he claimed vaguely, waving his be-ringed fingers in the air.

Sitric Silkbeard was impressed. He did not doubt that the earl could do what he said. Like Brian Boru, the earl of Orkney had a reputation that did not depend wholly on facts, but owed a lot to clever propaganda. To show that he would be an equally worthy partner in the enterprise, Sitric suggested that the invasion fleet arrive in Dublin Bay on Palm Sunday. He pointed out that Brian Boru had spent years building up a reputation for piety and giving generous gifts to the Church. Such an exceptionally devout Christian surely would be reluctant to fight a battle during the season of Easter. That attitude was bound to affect his followers, which would give the invaders an advantage.

Although Earl Sigurd and many of his followers were also Christians, their Viking blood did not baulk at fighting on holy days. Sitric Silkbeard, half North-man himself, felt the same way. He assured the earl that Maelmora would be just as willing to go to battle as they were. The king of Leinster would do anything to be rid of Brian Boru.

Sigurd the Stout was well satisfied with the plan. Sitric's previous defeats in battles against Malachy and Brian were known in the Viking world, but this time, and with so many allies, the earl was confident that things would be different. The forces arrayed against the Árd Rí were sure to win decisively. All of western Europe would bow before their supremacy. The Vikings, who ensured the victory, would gain incalculable treasure and a perfect base for future trade, as well as more land – a lot more land. Well watered, heavily timbered land, with fat cattle feeding on the grasslands, beautiful women waiting to be enjoyed by real men, monasteries full of gold and silver ... the earl's eyes gleamed at the thought. To go viking again! And with such glory waiting. Such an army as no man had seen before was about to be formed.

They would show their gratitude to Sitric Silkbeard, the earl promised. Sitric's share of the spoils would make him the richest man in a transformed Ireland. Sitric liked the sound of that. He would be just as happy under a Viking overlord as a Gaelic one; it did not matter so long as his treasury was filled. The earl of Orkney and the king of Dublin concluded their discussions in a rosy glow of mutual satisfaction.

While Sitric's longships were still within sight, Sigurd the Stout made himself busy. He organised fleets of envoys to summon warriors from the farthest reaches of his influence. He also charged his three oldest sons, Sumarlide, Bruce, and Einer Wrymouth, to rule his domain during his absence. As yet, Sigurd's newly arrived child bride by Malcolm of Scotland had given him no sons, but he promised he would lay all the plunder of Ireland at her feet when he returned from the invasion. He probably neglected to mention that he would have to kill the girl's grandfather to get it. Or that he expected to bring Gormlaith back with him, a woman who would demand a place as queen.

Such trivial matters were hardly worth considering in light of the advantages to be gained by victory in Ireland.

After he left the earl of Orkney, Sitric did not sail

back to Dublin immediately. First he made landfall on the Isle of Man, which was the stronghold of a pair of notorious pirates. The one known as Brodir claimed to be a supporter of Sigurd the Stout, but like most pirates his only real allegiance was to himself. The other pirate leader, Ospak, may have been his brother. The two had sailed the northern seas for years, sometimes together, always viking.

Brodir was Sitric's contingency plan. If Sigurd the Stout failed in his mission, the king of Dublin felt certain that Brodir would succeed. The taciturn Dane was famed both for his ruthlessness and his reputed knowledge of sorcery. Sitric made him exactly the same offer he had made to the earl of Orkney, stressing that Brian had to be killed. Brodir did little more than grunt in response, but the expression in his eyes was enough. He agreed to everything. Including Gormlaith.

Gormlaith frankly did not care whom she married next, as long as the Árd Rí was dead first. This was not a case of her Christian conscience avoiding a bigamous marriage. Under Brehon law Gormlaith had wed Brian without hesitation while he was still married to Duvcholly. Now she just wanted him slaughtered.

Melodramatic as it seems, this whole episode is corroborated by the Norse history of the Orkneys. According to them, it was Gormlaith who had suggested recruiting Brodir.

Brodir did not bother to inform the earl of Orkney about his own arrangement with Sitric Silkbeard. If everything happened as Brodir hoped, Sigurd the Stout would meet with an unfortunate accident on the field of battle and leave the way clear for Brodir to reap all the rewards. He did divulge his plans to Ospak, however. He intended to take twenty shiploads of warriors to Ireland and expected Ospak to provide another ten. Thirty ships from the Isle of Man! Imagine the plunder they would bring home!

Whether they were brothers or just colleagues, Brodir did not know Ospak as well as he thought he did. The conspiracy against Brian Boru was making Ospak extremely uncomfortable. For years he had listened with wholehearted admiration to stories about the Irish king. Brian seemed to be everything that Ospak himself would like to be. As the conspiracy gathered speed he began making different preparations. Ospak was his own man.

• • • • • • •

CHAPTER SEVEN

CALL TO ARMS

A t Kincora Brian was aware of the storm clouds gathering. Ever since the old outlaw days in the hills of Clare he had relied on a network of trustworthy runners to gather news for him. The bog and forest which blanketed much of Ireland made it all but impossible for a man to know what was going on even twenty miles away, but Brian had long since solved that problem. Fleet-footed messengers and deep-lunged shouters on hilltops kept him well informed. He knew which of the Leinster tribes were loyal to Maelmora and which were, if not disloyal to their king, at least wavering.

It was no surprise to Brian to learn that Maelmora and Sitric were conspiring against him yet again, combining their armies and calling on their allies throughout

Ireland. The two kings had the limited vision common to their time. They thought only in terms of what they could get for themselves. They envied the Árd Rí's successes which they could not emulate, and hated him for the riches and power which were his but not theirs.

In the season of Christmas an unexpected visitor appeared at the main gates of Kincora. The stranger had sailed a fleet of ten Viking longships up the Shannon and beached them below Béal Boru. When he answered the challenge of the high king's sentries by identifying himself as Ospak, from the Isle of Man, and further claimed he was a friend of Brian Boru, he and his party were ushered into the palace immediately. At sword's point.

We can imagine Brian's initial suspicion of an unknown Northman accompanied by two hundred warriors. But he was willing to listen. After offering the strangers warm water for washing and ale or buttermilk for drinking – the initial hospitality required under any conditions – Brian gave Ospak his undivided attention.

The pirate described in detail the plans for the invasion of Ireland, holding nothing back. He said that Brodir's warriors were heavily armed and already sleeping aboard their twenty ships at night. Ospak added that he did not want to be involved in going to war against such a good man, but Brodir had kept pressuring him. Reluctantly,

Ospak had gathered enough warriors to fill ten ships and taken them to an inlet on the other side of the harbour from Brodir's. Ospak's oldest son was with them.

Then he told an amazing story. One night a great commotion was heard in the sky above Brodir's ships. Startled awake, the men hastily seized their weapons – just in time to be drenched with a shower of boiling blood. They covered themselves with their shields but in spite of this many were scalded. The shower of blood lasted until sunrise. The following day a man died on each one of Brodir's ships.

On the second night there was another terrifying attack. This time it consisted of the Vikings' own weapons leaping out of their hands and scabbards, and striking one another in mid-air. The following day one man died on each of Brodir's ships. The third night, while the frightened and exhausted men tried in vain to sleep, an army of ravens attacked them from the sky, rending and tearing their flesh with iron claws. The following day yet another man died on every ship.

Brodir, furious and secretly terrified, went to Ospak and asked what this could possibly mean. Ospak replied that it was a warning from his pagan gods to give up the enterprise. Brodir angrily refused. That same day, Ospak and his warriors had slipped out of the harbour, although

Brodir tried to stop them, and set sail for Ireland.

Brian may have felt a shiver go up his spine at Ospak's story, but he did not doubt the truth of it. The Gael were as superstitious as the Northmen. Already the battle to come was attracting bad omens – and old women and young warriors were experiencing visitations.

At the conclusion of his narrative Ospak said he had come to Ireland to fight for a man whose nobility meant more to him than his own Viking heritage. To demonstrate his sincerity he brought forward his son, and requested that they both be baptised in the Christian faith by Brian's priest. It was done as he asked. And Ospak and his company were welcomed into Brian's army to fight side by side with the warriors of the Gael.

As the cold of winter stubbornly dragged on, Brian Boru made ready for one more battle. It cannot have been easy. He had thought the days of fighting were behind him; he had hoped he could enjoy the peace he had constructed. But this was Ireland, and war was again on the wind.

As always, Brian would have overall command of the army. His three oldest sons would receive choice assignments. Murrough – now known to friend and enemy alike as the Yew of Ros, after the famous tree that had yielded Maelmora to him – would be senior officer under the high king. Together with Flann and Conor, he would command the armies of Thomond, the most successful warriors in Munster.

Brian appointed his next son to remain at Kincora and administer affairs in his absence. Tadhg, whose mother was Achra, was a serious, level-headed man who could be relied upon to remain steady no matter what happened. Brian's family and numerous grandchildren would be safe in his care. Until the victory was won and the triumphant warriors came home again.

From Kincora the call to arms went out. The season of the warrior had arrived half a year too early – summer was the traditional time for battle. But in 1014, the first three months of the year were fully occupied with gathering and consolidating armies. The northern Uí Néill were conspicuous by their absence. It was too late for any further conciliatory gestures in their direction anyway.

One of the princes of the Uí Néill did respond favourably. Malachy Mór welcomed Brian's messengers to Dun na Sciath and fed them lavishly on venison and honeycomb. They returned to Kincora praising the generosity of the former high king. They also brought his pledge of a thousand warriors.

From before dawn until long after sundown, Brian was busy organising his army and planning his campaign. He had done it all before, so many times. Every detail must be worked out in advance, with contingencies to allow for unexpected problems. Brian had never fought a battle large or small that did not throw up some nasty surprises. He decided against taking his cavalry with him. The enemy they were going to face would be afoot. With a large number of men on the battlefield, horses would get in the way. He would limit them to mounts for himself and his most senior officers, plus one highly mobile band for which he had special plans: before the main body of his army reached Dublin, Brian planned to send his mounted warriors to ravage and burn the region north of the city. Dublin was the only actual town in this part of Ireland, but there were several tiny, outlying Norse settlements and some prosperous farms in the region known as Fingal (which means 'the fair foreigner'). The sight of scorched and smoking earth would greet the invaders as they came ashore. Brian had won more than one battle with what we today would call psychological warfare.

The days sped past. There were unsubstantiated rumours that the invasion fleet was already underway. The precincts of Kincora, which were capable of garrisoning three hundred warriors on a permanent basis, were stretched to capacity as tribal armies poured in from every part of Ireland. Hostages remaining in the guesting houses were summarily released and sent home. Their places were taken by chieftains and princes. The lawns around the palace were black with warriors who slept wrapped in their leather cloaks.

Brian was cheered to see the numbers of strong, eager young men – and not so young men – who hurried to Kincora to answer his call. He went out to greet each of his old allies as they arrived, to exchange news and views, to assure one another that all would be well, and to cast a calculating eye on the size and condition of the weaponry they brought with them. At the back of his mind was always the thought: would it be enough? Without the northern Uí Néill – and those in the south who chose to stand aside for their own reasons – could it be enough?

The ironsmiths at Kincora were kept working, even by torchlight. In battle the Gael employed a variety of weapons. The sword was standard and came in several styles: a leaf-shaped thrusting sword like the Roman *gladius*; a shorter instrument known as a dagger or dart; and a longer sword with a sharp edge and a sturdy hilt decorated with precious metals or animal teeth. The first two types were preferred for close combat. The longer weapon was indicative of high status and usually reserved for single combat. Brian Boru, who was a tall man, wielded a sword over half his height in length. The hilt reputedly was made of alloyed gold and set with jewels.

Irish battle spears came in several sizes, each with its own descriptive name, and were used both for thrusting and for casting. Their heads were of bronze or iron, made to a high standard. Some were broad and flat, others had a needle-sharp point. Still others were shaped like leaves with slightly rippled edges that would leave an even more grievous wound when they were pulled from the body. An exceptionally cruel weapon was a spear with a forked head and sharp, sickle-shaped barbs on both sides, reputedly modelled on the famed *Gae Bulga* of Cúchulainn. Unfortunately, no examples of this have ever been found by archaeologists. The annalists describe the Irish spears that were used at Clontarf as 'glittering, well-riveted, empoisoned, with well-shaped, beautiful handles fashioned of white hazel.'

Another weapon of awesome power was the mace. This consisted of a solid iron ball, usually spiked, to which a chain was attached. The other end of the chain was fastened to a sturdy wooden handle. One swing of the mace could send it crashing through a wall. The mace was heavy and awkward; most warriors preferred the axe. However the basic Irish axe, which had been in use since the Bronze Age, was being superseded by the end of the tenth century. Under Brian Boru the Gael were learning to use the terrifying Lochlann axe made famous by the Vikings. There was only one way to use the Viking battle axe. It had to be held in both hands and swung from the shoulder with a man's full weight behind it. But when it struck, it killed.

The sword was the more versatile weapon. It might be used right-handed or left, or tossed from one hand to the other. Depending on the shape, it could slice, slash or thrust. In the case of the long sword, the enemy could be hit with the flat of the blade and knocked off balance or even stunned. Some warriors boasted that they kept their swords sharp enough to shave off a man's beard.

A very different weapon with an ancient provenance was the sling, the early Irish version of artillery. This consisted of a flexible pole with a leather sling affixed to one end. A heavy stone placed in the sling was propelled with great force by a skilful whipping motion of the pole. In the right hands, the pole-sling was deadly, even at a distance – weapons experts have speculated that this was what David employed against Goliath.

The shields carried by Brian's army were circular in shape, made of stout Irish oak cross-braced and edged with iron. They were covered with leather dyed in brilliant colours, and bossed with bronze which had been plated in gleaming brass. These were not full length, whole-body shields, but carried on the arm to allow the warrior maximum agility.

The Gael did not wear armour in battle. At most, warriors protected their upper torsos with coats of specially toughened leather. By the end of the tenth century a few may have possessed metal corselets in imitation of the Northmen, but there is no record of any of the Irish troops wearing armour at Clontarf. The often cited 'portrait' of Brian Boru, which was first published in 1726 by Bazaleal Creake and used in Geoffrey Keating's *General History of Ireland*, shows him wearing a spiky crown and solid body armour like one of King Arthur's knights in a Hollywood movie. This image is not only an anachronism but a total fantasy.

Gaelic warriors either wore their hair long, or elaborately braided. If it was long, they might wear close-fitting leather helmets to keep the hair out of their eyes when they fought, but leather was no protection against a sword or an axe. For that they must trust in God and their own skill.

Estimates have wildly exaggerated the number of warriors who fought at the Battle of Clontarf, but it is safe to say there were probably at least seven to eight thousand on each side. As was customary at the time, Brian organised his combined forces into three large *catha* – battalions or divisions – which were then subdivided into companies of a hundred warriors each. The highest-ranking kings commanded the battalions; lesser nobles were in charge of the companies. Leaders were appointed for every band of nine warriors, so that each group would be like a little tribe.

Officers of every rank were expected to fight side by side with their men. In the heat of battle even kings received no special consideration.

Ignoring his age, his weariness, and the ache in his joints, Brian was out amongst the warriors every day, in all weathers. His sons worried about him. They noticed what he refused to admit: that it was difficult for him. But these were his men and he must do everything possible to prepare them. As always, up until the last moment Brian worried that he might have forgotten something vital. Then there was no time left. It looked like there would be enough men – there must be enough; he did not know how large the enemy force would be but this *must* be enough!

Brian had been waiting, undoubtedly anxious, for news of Malachy Mór's intentions. He must have been very relieved when Malachy and his personal army arrived at Kincora. A celebratory feast was cut short to allow for a night's sleep, and on the following morning the combined armies of the two kings got underway. The annalists report it was the feast day of St Patrick.

As they set out for their rendezvous with fate, the Gael were attired in the bright colours beloved of their race. The more colours, the higher the wearer's status. The Book of Rights describes the costume of the noble class: '... cloaks of white, red, blue, green, deep purple, variegated, plaid of lasting colour, cloaks of strength, fair cloaks with borders not crooked, cloaks with golden borders and ring-clasps, others bordered with white, and napped cloaks trimmed with purple.'

Princes and chieftains also wore 'white, glossy shirts and colourful, well-adjusted, enfolding tunics over comfortable long vests'. These garments were made of the finest silk and linen. Trimmings of woven gold were not uncommon. Some also had helmets described as 'golden' – perhaps brass plates affixed to leather and set with precious stones. A man of high rank might wear a heavy gold torc around his neck, not only testifying to his wealth but also useful for absorbing an unexpected blow. His long cloak was made of densely woven, brilliantly dyed wool, lined with fur or with silk purchased from Norse traders. The massive brooch that fastened the cloak was precisely arranged with the sharp point sticking up at an angle, ready to stab the hand of an unsuspecting assailant who reached over his shoulder.

Gaelic warriors below the chieftainly class were clothed in tunics of saffron-dyed wool, belted at the waist with leather or horsehair. An undyed linen undergarment was considered a necessity. The womenfolk sewed coloured fringe on the hems of the tunics, but once the march was underway the more experienced fighting men ripped it off. In close combat the fringe could be clutched by an opponent and used to hold the wearer long enough for the killing blow. Young Gaelic men, who were vain about their legs, went to war barelegged, wearing a short, snugly fitted jacket and a 'battle apron' which extended only to mid-thigh. This garment, often made of plaid, was the forerunner to the kilt of the Scottish highlands.

Older men preferred full-length woollen trews, narrow at the calves and with a strap over the instep to hold them in place, or snugly woven hose crossbound with leather thongs. Their shoes were made of robust rawhide. They too possessed cloaks, although these were usually made of leather. Several layers of greased deer-skin would keep a man dry in the rain and serve him for a bed at night.

Every company had its place in the line of march, shoulder to shoulder as Brian wanted, his loyal tribes together with their allies. The battle they faced would not be the Irish against the Vikings, as it is usually and simplistically described. It was not even pagan against Christian. It would be Irish and Viking against Viking and Irish. Inside their skins the various races of mankind are much alike, and in 1014 there was little to choose between one group of combatants or the other. What would make the difference, what always makes the difference, was the quality of their leaders.

On a brisk March morning Brian Boru's army crossed the Shannon at the ford below Kincora and headed northeast. Murrough, now forty-three years of age, rode beside his father at the head of the Dalcassians. But all eyes were fixed on the Árd Rí. A tall old man sitting straight as a pine tree on the back of a prancing horse, with no fear in his eyes or his heart. His great sword was at his hip. That was what the men needed to see: Brian Boru able and ready for battle.

Murrough had been thoroughly briefed in Brian's battle plans. So had his brothers, Conor and Flann. Even if one of them fell, the others knew their father's mind and would see that the other officers adhered to the strategy he had so carefully worked out. It was crucial to ensure that the battle had a definite shape and a pre-ordained conclusion. The discipline Brian had worked so hard to instil in his army was about to be tested as never before.

There were chieftains and warriors Brian could not control, and he knew it. In the fever of battle everything could go terribly wrong.

Throughout the march Brian held open a place of honour in the front rank for the former high king, and had an exceptionally fine horse waiting for him. But Malachy did not take it. He rode on his own horse in the very midst of his warriors, with an attendant leading his spare mount, an unbroken stallion from Meath. The army from Meath was supported by a large force from Waterford, Hiberno-Norse warriors loyal to Brian.

The middle ranks of the marchers were occupied by warriors from Tipperary and the midlands, some Leinstermen who had decided to stand with Brian after all, kings from Oriel and Fermanagh, Ospak and his men, and southern Gaelic tribes such as the Decies. A contingent of the Hiberno-Norse from Limerick was followed by a troop of sturdy warriors from Connacht. The current king of Connacht, a son of Cathal Ua Connor, had for his own reasons declined to join Brian. But other Connachtmen did. Brian entrusted them with guarding the rear – a position of the greatest danger which offered a splendid opportunity for valour.

Murrough was bringing his own son, Turlough, to take

part in the first great battle of his life. Turlough was only fifteen, but that was the age for taking up arms – in the eleventh century a boy was considered a man at fifteen. Another who was almost but not quite fifteen was Donough, Brian's son by Gormlaith. The boy was eager to fight but Brian was not willing to see him on the battlefield yet. Instead, he put Donough in charge of a cavalry troop assigned to forage for provisions to re-supply the main army. The boy chafed at the assignment; he resented being kept away from the excitement, the thrilling glory he imagined. By the time he finally reached Clontarf he would be thirsting for blood.

In the years following the Battle of Clontarf, men from every Gaelic clan in Ireland would claim to have fought with Brian Boru. Not all of them did. Some never received the summons. Others promised to come, then failed to do so. There were those who simply could not see anything in it for themselves and forgot the whole idea. But enough of the Gael assembled to take part in the march from Kincora to Clontarf – and earn themselves a place in history.

Once they crossed the Shannon and entered Leinster, Brian's army was in enemy territory. No matter how they approached Dublin, they would have to go through Leinster. Dublin was, in effect, a kingdom within a kingdom, surrounded on three sides by Leinster. On the fourth side was the sea.

Brian Boru was giving a lot of thought to the sea.

The battle to come was on the minds of other men as well. Brian's royal son-in-law, King Malcolm of Scotland, was fully occupied defending the Scottish borders against both Northmen and Saxons, but when he learned of the upcoming invasion he had despatched a company of highlanders to go to Brian's aid. These were led by Donald, Great Steward of Marr, chieftain of a branch of the Owenacht tribe that had settled in Scotland, and Murray, the Great Steward of Lennox. They would reach the northeast coast of Ireland in time to march south and meet Brian Boru's forces during Holy Week. These welcome reinforcements would have given Brian some comfort had he known about them in advance, but he probably did not. He had to rely on what he had, including the battalion that had accompanied Malachy Mór to Kincora.

A millennium later it is impossible to know just what Brian felt about the former high king, the man he had displaced. They had been enemies and they had been allies, but in Brian's mind there must have been a question about Malachy. He was seven years younger than Brian and he had more time left to him. If Brian died in the battle to come it would be to Malachy's advantage. He probably would be asked to resume his high kingship. Malachy was a Christian and not a bad man; Brian did not believe the Meathman wished him ill. Yet who could say what he might do when opportunity beckoned? Brian Boru had never hesitated to make the most of his own opportunities.

The army's route took it more than halfway across Ireland, climbing hills, fording streams, skirting treacherous bogs and pushing through dense forests that would have been impassable but for the roads that had been cut by Brian Boru. To follow the line of march today one would pass near the towns of Nenagh, Roscrea, Portlaoise, Kildare, and Naas before reaching the western outskirts of Dublin. By automobile on the motorway it is a pleasant drive of some three hours, allowing a brief stop for lunch. For thousands of foot soldiers carrying their battle gear, living off the land as much as they could and coping with mud and uncertain weather, it could take several days.

During the course of the march the officers met every night to discuss the matters uppermost in their minds, which ranged from provisions to armaments to the physical condition of the troops. Malachy Mór always appeared for these conferences, but made few contributions. The man with a reputation for conviviality had little to say. When the Árd Rí tried to find subjects for conversation that would draw him out, the former high king seemed disinterested.

Whatever thoughts were on his mind, Malachy did not share them with Brian Boru.

CHAPTER EIGHT

THE DRAGONS ARE COMING

True to his word, Sigurd the Stout recruited a number of Viking princes to join his invasion fleet. The Western Isles contributed a great number of warriors, as did Scandinavian colonies elsewhere. The Viking network was not cohesive but it was expansive, stretching from Iceland to the fringes of Russia. It also was, for its time, highly mobile. The longships which left the sheltered harbour at Scapa Flow sailed to almost every shore known to be occupied by Northmen, Vikings who would be eager to plunder Ireland.

Viking ships were a miracle of maritime design. The best were clinker-built of weathered oak planks, affixed with large iron nails and caulked with wool or animal hair and pitch. The vessels were wide through the body but swooped upwards at prow and stern to form an elegant curve. The deck was constructed of pine for lighter weight, fitted with rowing benches on either side and a gangway down the middle. Rollers to be used in beaching were stowed lengthwise under the seats. The warriors, who doubled as oarsmen, slept on their benches. All toilet facilities were over the side.

The bottom was flat amidships, where a tiny cabin offered what little protection was available from wind and wave. A leather cover could be pulled over the occupants, who would have been only the ranking officers or perhaps fragile cargo. Below the waterline the construction was strong yet flexible, in order to give with the force of the waves. A stepped mast held a large, square sail sewn of heavy linen, which could be raised or lowered by means of a tackle on the forestay. The deep keel was some twenty centimetres thick, broad in the centre but gradually diminishing towards the sternpost. This not only maintained stability in rough water but also permitted the use of the sail on open sea, greatly increasing range and speed.

The nearest equivalent may have belonged to the ancient Phoenicians. The remains of a Phoenician ship with what appears to be a seagoing keel were discovered off the Azores in the twentieth century. The Romans, for all their ingenuity, had nothing so clever; even their fabled triremes, with three rows of oars, were coaster boats.

For all its technical excellence, the Viking ship was most famous for the dragonheaded prow. This was the terrifying object the Christian monks first saw emerging from the sea mist. Not every seagoing vessel boasted such an emblem; it was reserved for the 'Dragon' class warships, which also had the dragon's tail on the stern. But most Viking vessels were ornamented in some fashion. Like the Gael, even the lowest Northman had an innate love of beauty.

While he waited impatiently in his stronghold in the Orkneys, Sigurd the Stout was not thinking of beauty – or if he was, it was the beauty of the treasure he hoped to take from Ireland. He did not have long to wait; boats soon began arriving. The fierce fighting men of the Shetlands and the Hebrides were the first to join the Orkneymen, but within days contingents appeared from what is modern-day Cornwall, Flanders and parts of England. Men whose names were famous in the northern lands flocked to the Orkneys to take part in what promised to be a great adventure. Among them were several chieftains from the Hebrides, who were friends and allies of Sigurd's: an intrepid explorer called Hrafn the Red, who claimed to have travelled 'to the ends of the earth', and recently had converted to Christianity; the wealthy Erling of Straumey, who was eager to supply additional weaponry for the undertaking; and Thorstein, son of Hall of the Side. Some years earlier Thorstein had come to the Orkneys from Iceland with his friend Flosi, who was now a trusted retainer of Earl Sigurd. Every person who entered Sigurd's hall was met by Flosi first.

The women did their part. To them fell the task of sharpening the weapons and rubbing the chainmail armour with fat until every link glistened. Sigurd's elderly mother presented her favourite son with a new banner which she had sewn herself, a bright yellow flag featuring a black raven, the favourite symbol of Wotan, god of war. When the wind blew it looked as if the raven on the banner was flapping its wings. 'You will be safe under those wings,' the old woman promised Sigurd.

At about the same time, a supernatural vision of Earl Sigurd with blood on his face appeared to the inhabitants of the Orkneys. A man who knew him well saw him approaching on a horse and hurried forward to offer aid, thinking the earl was injured – before he could speak the figure vanished into thin air. A similar vision was reported by crofters and goatherds and an old woman spreading her washing on the ground to dry.

Prophesiers as far away as Iceland rolled the bones and reported that an horrific battle soon to be fought would destroy 'all the brave men of the North'. But the dark omens which had not been enough to dissuade Brodir did not deter Sigurd either. He trusted in his mother's promise.

While he waited for the day chosen to embark, the earl strolled down to the harbour many times to admire his assembled fleet. His personal ship, the flag ship that would carry his banner, was the most prepossessing of all. The fabric of the single sail which now lay folded in the stern was boldly striped in purple and yellow. The gunwales were painted in discordant shades that would appear garish to the modern eye, while the sides of the vessel were ornamented with carved wooden images of cavorting dolphins and leaping stags. The most thrilling figure of all was the immense dragon head on the prow. It was painted in brilliant crimson and gold, complete with cruel fangs and flaring nostrils. Although its jet black eyes were made of polished stones, they seemed alive with an insane fury.

When he saw his ship Sigurd felt the pride of a man admiring his firstborn son.

Like Brian Boru, the earl took inventory of the

weaponry which would be at his disposal. The Scandinavians were arriving well armed. Their skilfully made swords were larger than the average Irish sword. Norse examples which have been discovered by archaeologists measure between sixty-one and eighty-one centimetres long. Some had only one sharpened edge; others had two. These were the heavy two-handed swords which almost rivalled the axe in destructiveness. The pommel and guard of the swordhilt was sometimes ornamented with neatly inlaid pieces of gold, silver and copper. By the eleventh century many of the Norse were literate, and inscribed their swords not only with ogham runes invoking the aid of pagan gods, but with prayers in Latin, beseeching Christ's support.

Iron-headed lances were carried into battle, but only as part of an initial assault. They were too awkward in close-quarter encounters. Shields were made almost entirely of wood, with a heavy bronze boss in the middle to protect the hand holding the shield.

Pride of place among Viking weaponry belonged to the Lochlann battleaxe, another weapon made to be used two-handed. The heavy iron heads were perfectly weighted and took a sharp edge. It was claimed that a powerful axeman could slice through an opponent's neck, then on the backstroke slice through both legs just below the knee. Reputedly the unfortunate victim fell in three parts before he knew he was dead!

Body armour was a distinguishing feature of the Vikings. Warriors fortunate enough to follow a wealthy lord were outfitted with hauberks, long coats of bluish-green chainmail links that reached to the knee. The sleeves were usually short, although sometimes long enough to cover the hands. Beneath their hauberks the men had padded coats to protect their skin from the bite of the metal links. They wore metal helmets which were conical in shape and fitted with a nose piece, a long narrow strip riveted to the forehead of the helmet and extending over the end of the nose. Viking helmets did not have large cattle horns attached to them – this is a modern convention beloved of cartoonists who do not realise what a liability it would be in battle, when an opponent might grasp the horns and twist off his adversary's head.

Graphic illustrations of Viking armour being worn by Norman warriors are found on the famous Bayeux Tapestry. This masterpiece was commissioned by the half-brother of William the Conqueror shortly after William's historic victory at the Battle of Hastings in 1066. The tapestry depicts the entire event in vivid detail. As an interesting footnote to history, the successful invasion which would shape the destiny of England for centuries to come, and affect Ireland as well, involved a second-generation Viking – the half-Danish Harold Godwine – fighting and losing to a third-generation Viking, William, duke of Normandy. 'Norman' is a corruption of 'Norseman', and was the name given to the Vikings who settled in France.

As Earl Sigurd and his auxiliaries made ready for what they expected to be the successful invasion of Ireland, Brodir was putting the finishing touches on his own contribution to the army. This included a thousand Viking mercenaries equipped with chainmail armour. They were under the command of an exceptionally brutal Norseman called Anrud, a son of Elbric Long Ears. Anrud was reputed to be the only man on earth whom Brodir himself feared.

Neither the Vikings nor the Irish were known for their ability as archers; both primarily used the bow and arrow as hunting weapons. But Brodir equipped some of his men with bows and poisoned arrows. The dark Dane had made one fortune from his violent enterprises and he was determined to make another. Like ravens scavenging a battlefield, he and his warriors were going to carry away the spoils of Ireland.

Come what may, Brodir was determined that Sigurd

the Stout would not be taking Gormlaith back to the Orkneys.

The earl was of a different opinion. While the invasion fleet seemed to increase exponentially he had found time to fit out a special apartment close to his own royal quarters. It was fitted with furs and silks and feather-stuffed beds, lamps and candles and bronze braziers to keep a princess warm. Sigurd had never met an Irish princess and had no idea what one would like, but that did not matter. She would live as he dictated. She would be his trophy. The sagas would tell of Sigurd and Gormlaith for generations to come.

Sigurd the Stout was a happy man. It was as if Valhalla itself were about to open its gates and welcome him inside. The morning of departure for Ireland was the best morning of his life.

They sailed out with the tide. Earl Sigurd was standing in the prow of the lead vessel with one hand on the dragon's head. Above him the raven banner whipped in a rising wind. Black wings opening and closing. When the earl turned to look back he could see a vast flotilla following him. Every sail was raised, every ship was crowded with men. Boasting, laughing, shouting raucous insults at one another.

It was like the old days, Sigurd thought, before the White

Christ. These were the days of Red Thor come again.

Their journey took them south out of Scapa Flow, into Pentland Firth, then into the dark and treacherous waters of the Atlantic. As they approached the ocean the wind changed. It blasted down upon them to such an extent that sail was not only useless but dangerous. The rowers bent to their oars with all their strength, fighting to keep the ships to their course.

Past Dunnet Head and Strathy Point and the treacherous waters of Cape Wrath. Beaching the boats only to sleep. Then away again. South along the Minch and the Little Minch and then the Sea of the Hebrides, where they were joined by the fleet of the Hebrideans.

As they made their way amongst the Western Isles other vessels sallied out to join them. Three or four were longships, but most were small fishing boats or simple dugout canoes. They could not hope to make the entire journey but they wanted to be a little part of it, to sit by their fires and boast of having sailed with Sigurd of Orkney. Only once in a lifetime, but well worth living for!

The earl was beginning to be concerned. So many warriors were following the raven flag and expecting a share in the reward: would there be enough to satisfy them all? Would there even be a battle? Brian Boru was surely an old man by now. When he saw the size of the force arrayed against him, would he run and take his army with him? If that happened, would Sigurd's followers turn against him in frustration? They were expecting a glorious battle. All their pent-up aggression would seek an outlet. Men disappointed in their expectations had destroyed their leaders before.

The dragonships passed Skye, Islay, approached the Mull of Kintyre. The keenest noses among them began to catch hints of some verdant fragrance. Green and growing things: grass and tree and flower. It was better than the most exotic perfume to men who had been so long at sea. Salt pustules on their exposed skin, salt caked in their heavy beards, unremitting cold and shrieking wind and a running sea and then ... there was Ireland! Over there, on your right, do you see? Strong green shoulders breaking through the mist? A great cheer went up.

The voyage was not over yet. Before they reached Dublin they made landfall on the Isle of Man. The island was in the middle of the Irish Sea, almost equidistant from the Mountains of Mourne in Ireland and western Northumbria in Britain, and the ideal place to make any last-minute repairs to the ships and take fresh water aboard.

When Brodir's men saw the great fleet approaching in the distance they ran to tell him the news. Soon twenty longships were gliding out from their harbour. Standing in the prow of the lead vessel with its own dragon head, Brodir shouted a hoarse greeting to Sigurd the Stout.

Sigurd was not surprised to see him. He had never doubted that Brodir would join him. But his was a tainted pleasure. He had all the allies he needed already; twenty more ships full of warriors would only dilute his share of the plunder. And Brodir, whom he knew of old, would demand a share the equal of the earl's. Sigurd shrugged; he would deal with that problem when the time came. Perhaps a knife in the old pirate's ribs when no-one was looking. Who would notice one more dead man on a battlefield?

Sigurd pasted a welcoming grin on his face and shouted a return greeting to Brodir. 'Lie alongside,' he cried, 'and we'll feast tonight!'

• • • • • • •

CHAPTER NINE

THE WEEK BEFORE

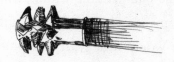

Earl Sigurd and the invasion fleet sailed into Dublin Bay on Palm Sunday, as agreed. The bay slowly turned black with ships. The king of Dublin and his entourage went down to the shore to observe their arrival. It was the first time Sitric Silkbeard had seen the full might of the Western Isles and their allies, and he was awestruck. He returned to his palace to tell Gormlaith that Brian Boru was as good as dead. Then he ordered a great banquet to be prepared for the Scandinavian leaders.

Sitric prudently asked his mother to stay in her quarters during the feast. He feared that Gormlaith's appearance would provoke an exchange between the earl and the pirate that would damage his own credibility. 'Viking men do not eat with their women,' he told her, 'and we must not offer them insult.' Gormlaith herself may have felt insulted by this remark, but she agreed to her son's request. It was important that all went well.

Satisfied that she would not cause any trouble on this particular occasion, Sitric busied himself overseeing final preparations. His stronghold must be at least as impressive as that belonging to the earl of Orkney.

In 1014 Dublin in its entirety was south of the Liffey. A timber bridge near present-day Bridgefoot Street connected the city on the southern bank of the river with the open fields on the northern side. The bridge, which later came to be known as Dubhgall's Bridge, consisted of a gangway supported by rows of wooden piles sunk deep in the marshy ooze between the tidal waters of the bay and the Black Pool. When the tide came in, the bridge was submerged.

The king's palace stood approximately where Dublin Castle stands now. Sedimentary evidence suggests that areas such as today's Merrion Square were often underwater as a result of tidal flooding, and to avoid this problem royal residences had been built and re-built on the high ground first claimed by Ivarr the Boneless. By the eleventh century the palace comprised a large cluster of timber and wicker rectangles roofed with thatch.

Following the custom of the time, the banqueting hall was unattached to any of the other buildings. Like the kitchens and the ovens it was kept separate for fear of fire.

In preparation for his guests Sitric Silkbeard had ordered his servants to drape the walls of the banqueting hall with swathes of eastern silk. They had piled every available surface with items of gold and silver to attest to the wealth at his command. Here he waited anxiously, nervously, for the arrival of his guests.

The invasion fleet passed between the tiny island known as Ireland's Eye and the grassy isthmus of Sutton, then circled around Howth Head to the landward side. Hundreds of Viking vessels were drawn up onto the shores around Dublin Bay. The largest dragonships were at Howth, but others made landfall at Sutton, around the mouth of the Liffey, and as far south as Sandymount.

When all was in readiness, Sigurd and the northern chiefs sailed from Howth to Dublin Harbour. They took the precaution of bringing armed bodyguards with them. By 1014 some Vikings had adopted the habit of bath-ing, but those in the invasion force had not washed their bodies for weeks: their odour came ahead of them on the wind from the sea.

The king of Dublin welcomed them to his palace

with a full range of Danish formalities. He was relieved to see that Brodir and Earl Sigurd apparently were on friendly terms. Sigurd introduced Amlaff, the son of the king of Lochlann, by saying, 'This man brings two thousand Danmarkians with him. They are hard warriors like Brodir here; they have no reverence for God or for man, for Church or for sanctuary.' Amlaff fingered the cross he wore on a thong around his neck, and smiled. Coldly.

Sitric gave only casual mention to the absent Maelmora. He told the earl, 'The king of Leinster is in the south, collecting an army which will join us here shortly. Of course my Danes are quite capable of persecuting the battle on their own – with your assistance, of course,' he added with an unctuous smile. Things were going better than he had hoped. Still no sign of his mother, fortunately. Sitric began to look forward to the evening ahead.

After a massive meal of roast meat and shellfish was devoured and the rush-covered floor of the banqueting hall was littered with scraps – eagerly snatched by the omnipresent Irish wolfhounds – the men settled down to discuss the upcoming battle. Sigurd said to his host, 'Brian Boru is not as good as you think he is. Even if he does stand to fight, which I doubt once he sees how great our numbers are, the battle will not last until midday. Your doddering old high king will be dead long before that, I assure you. Then we can all come back here and enjoy another feast.'

Brodir waited until the drinking horns had been drained several times before entering the conversation. The grim Dane did not often speak, but when he did he commanded attention. He announced that he had called upon his knowledge of the dark arts to obtain a prediction for the future. 'If we take to the battlefield on Good Friday the Irish king will die, but if we fight on any other day our men will surely be slain.'

'Then Good Friday it shall be!' cried Sitric Silkbeard. He shook his drinking horn in the air for emphasis, sloshing Danish beer over the men nearest to him.

It was a long, wet night. Maelmora of Leinster arrived the next day.

Brian Boru had his share of enemies, perhaps more than most. He was never a man to do things by half measures. The warriors following Maelmora's banner belonged to tribes that had been forced against their will to submit to Brian's authority. Their grudges against him dated back to his earliest days as king of Munster. The present counties of Waterford, Wexford, Carlow, Wicklow and Kildare would be well represented amongst the rebels. With them were those Norsemen who had not already given their allegiance to Brian.

While Maelmora was gathering his auxiliaries in the southeast he may have wished that Brian Boru had extended his road-building fervour to that remote corner of Leinster. But no; preferential treatment was given to Munster. Preferential treatment was always given to Munster. Maelmora had ground his teeth and dreamed of the day he would even the score.

The expanse from Clonmel to Waterford and then to Dublin had not been easy travelling. The rivers were deep and fast-running, the foothills were smothered beneath dense forest, and the heights were covered with broken granite or blanket bog. Wexford was a wild and dangerous place away from the coast. It was known to be the haunt of wolves and evil spirits. In Wicklow there was hardly any human settlement in the upper reaches of the hill country, although local tribes lived well on the revenue they creamed from St Kevin's monastery at Glendalough.

Along the way Maelmora had added a new chieftain to his army: Domnall mac Ferghaile, king of the Fortuatha, Gaelic tribes who had intermarried with the Norse. When they reached Dublin some of Maelmora's followers fell to plundering the rich districts surrounding the city.

Maelmora assigned Domnall and his personal warriors to guard the strip of tidal mud in front of the city's palisades. Here the defensive bank had been extended by a mortared wall nine feet high and four and a half feet thick, and buttressed by offset stones.

Maelmora thought any further precautions would not be necessary for long. He agreed with the earl of Orkney that the battle itself would not last half a day. Battles never did. After the initial headlong assault the outcome was obvious within a few hours.

The king of Leinster allowed the rest of his army to settle down for the night, camping along the shores of the bay. They spread out across the sands, much as the foreign battle force was doing. Perhaps there was some discussion between them; perhaps the two contingents kept themselves apart out of pride. They would get to know each other well enough when the battle began.

With the day for battle agreed, Earl Sigurd retired to the Hill of Howth to wait with his fleet. To his mind the rounded summit rising from the sea was a more regal setting than Sitric's damp and mildewed palace beside the Liffey. The entire sweep of Dublin Bay could be viewed from the summit of Howth. What better command position before the battle began? When the fighting started the earl would be in the thick of it, of course.

The first man off the first dragonship.

Brodir had the same idea, but he kept it to himself.

Both the earl and Brodir – separately – had suggested to Sitric Silkbeard that they would like to meet Gormlaith in person sometime before the battle, but Sitric had managed to outmanoeuvre them. That was one mistake he was determined not to make.

Brian Boru did not intend to make any mistakes either. In his mind he kept going over and over the area around Dublin. Visualising it from different viewpoints. The size and strength of the enemy was an unknown quantity and would be so until the end; but he knew the land and the foreigners did not – the invasion force would be seeing it for the first time. Sitric and Maelmora were familiar with the environs of Dublin, but Brian was confident they had never actually studied it.

Few men studied the topography of a possible battlefield the way he did. Since his days as an outlaw in Clare he knew the land was the one ally he could always rely on.

The northern reaches of Dublin Bay, from the estuary of the Tolka extending toward the hill of Howth, consisted of crescent-shaped sands and short-lived sandbars. From the bay the land rose in a long, gradual slope towards Magh Dumha, translated as 'The Mound on the

Plain' – an area now called Phibsborough. A man might not realise there was a slope at all unless he walked it.

The Tolka ran northeast of Magh Dumha. Embedded in a green valley, it appeared to be a pleasant little river. In size the Tolka was no competition for its neighbour, the Liffey, but it was deep in places, with dark pools where wily brown trout hid. Eels and lampreys, which live in both fresh and saltwater, could be trapped at the weirs. A person viewing the Tolka today would find only a narrow brown thread of muddy water tamed by cement walls to facilitate the engineering required for a modern seaport. But it was not always so.

As Brian and his army approached Dublin the weather was a constant topic of conversation. Spring in Ireland was uncertain. Frost was frequent until the month of May; ice was less so, but even snow was possible. There would always be the rain, everything from a fine mist to a pelting downpour, saturating man and land alike and making mud the only certainty. The army had encountered plenty of that along the way. The warriors were tired; the Árd Rí had been pushing them hard. He could not be certain when the foreign invaders would arrive, although he had no doubt that Sitric and Maelmora knew.

Brian was planning his own welcome for the Vikings.

Long before his army reached Dublin he ordered his mounted warriors to ride north and despoil Fingal. Everything that would burn was to be put to the torch: a blazing pyre to warn the invaders what was waiting for them. He gave no order as to the disposition of the inhabitants. His men knew what he wanted: no living Norseman of fighting age left to join the enemy.

At last the Irish army came to a series of low hills that rolled across the land like the waves of the sea. Every hill had a long incline that set fire to the muscles in tired legs. Just one more step. And one more. Just one more hill ...

When they could see the walls of the city up ahead, Brian ordered the combined armies to prepare to camp for the night. The location he selected was part of a large area known as Kilmainham, named in honour of Saint Maighnenn, who had been both bishop and abbot there early in the seventh century. Originally Kilmainham occupied both sides of the Liffey, including the present-day Phoenix Park. The ground was somewhat elevated, with wooded bluffs above the tide line. In 1014 a small stone church built by the saint himself was still standing on a height overlooking the Liffey.

When Murrough's tent was pitched in a grove of trees on the southern bank of the river, Brian's son is said to have remarked on the serenity of the place. Murrough added, 'I should like to rest here after the battle.'

Malachy Mór and his men did not join Brian's encampment but made their own arrangements on the north side of the Liffey. Brian took note of this, but did not comment. It was what he would have done if the situations had been reversed. The former high king was still part of the defending force but was demonstrating that he was his own man as well.

Brian's army quickly set about making camp. Chopping wood and gathering deadfall for fires, fetching buckets of water from the river. Joking a little among themselves, to prove they were not as tired as they really were. The rising smoke from their cooking fires guided a party of unexpected allies to them. Just before dusk, and to his delighted surprise, Brian was joined by Donald, Great Steward of Marr, and Murray, Great Steward of Lennox, with two companies of their men. Brian immediately ordered food and drink for all, then sat down to hear their story.

Unfortunately the Scots brought bad news. The foreign invasion force had already arrived. They were planning to march inland on Good Friday, accompanied by Maelmora and the Danes of Dublin. Brian had hoped to wait until after Easter to give his army a chance to rest before facing combat. Now he learned that time had run out.

The Árd Rí reviewed his troops for the final time on Thursday morning, 22 April. An Irish chronicler described the combined armies as they marched before the high king: 'The battle phalanx, compact, huge, disciplined, moving in silence, mutely, bravely, haughtily, unitedly, with one mind. With three score and ten banners over them, of red, and of yellow, and of green, and of all kinds of colours.' (Upon reviewing his troops in their full military splendour during the American Civil War, the great general Robert E. Lee remarked, 'It is well that war is so terrible, or we should grow too fond of it.')

The warrior spirit of the Gael found poetry in war, in the moments of true beauty and transcendent courage which can briefly illuminate the arena of death. The same quality belonged to the Norse who would meet them on the battlefield. Both sides anticipated glory. Throughout human history it has been war, not peace, which seems irresistible to man.

Like all good generals before and after him, Brian Boru restricted the number of people who knew his precise battle plans. There was always the possibility of spies divulging critical information to the enemy. Therefore the final meeting of the army's leaders on the evening

before the battle comprised only the division commanders: Brian's three sons, and Malachy Mór. One high ranking officer not invited was Brian's own son-in-law, Cian.
While Brian might have total trust in Cian, that did not
extend to the Owenachts and Desmonians he was leading. Brian might forgive erstwhile enemies but he did
not turn his back to them at a crucial time.

Brian's sons opened the meeting by urging him to
relinquish command of the army in the morning and
retire to a safe vantage point. Perhaps this came as a surprise to him; perhaps he had been expecting it. He listened to their request, objected strenuously, and at last
promised he would stay clear of the conflict. 'Ireland
cannot spare you' was the winning argument, one Brian
could not contradict. His head, which contained not
only his plans for the battle but also for Ireland's future,
must be protected.

Brian appointed Murrough to lead the combined
armies in his stead. It was an unmistakeable declaration
of his confidence in his oldest son. Murrough, whom
the annals describe as fractious and headstrong, was also
rebellious on occasion, as sons often are. If ever there was
an opportunity to cement the relationship between the
two of them, this was it.

However, Brian's announcement provoked a furious outburst from Malachy Mór. The former high king angrily stalked away from the meeting and did not return that night. Nor, one may assume, did he hear the final outline of Brian's battle plans. Instead he returned to his own battalion of Meathmen.

If Brian was upset by Malachy's defection he did not show it. After many years of dealing with the shifting waters of Gaelic politics, he knew that status dictated the arrangement of forces. Accordingly he set them out. Each of the three battalions would be led by the highest ranking king. Murrough and the Dalcassians would comprise the front rank of the first battalion, because the Árd Rí's tribe must be the first to face the enemy. They would be supported by the princes of Munster, including the Owenachts and Desmonians under Cian's command.

The army would begin the battle with a centre and two wings. The orders would go down from the top through the chain of command, one of Brian's military innovations. The captains of the individual companies would be expected to enforce discipline, although there must be a degree of flexibility as the battle progressed. Brian believed in flexibility and initiative.

He announced these arrangements with calm confidence. The face he showed that evening was the face he had always shown.

When the entire plan was laid out before them, the men whom Brian trusted most must have felt relieved. The Árd Rí on his horse would not lead them into battle but he would still be with them in every way that mattered. As always, his would be the will that guided them. The experience, the courage ... and the guile.

From Kilmainham, Brian might not have been able to see the Viking fleet in the bay, but now he knew they were there, and in daunting numbers. Afterwards it was claimed that approximately a thousand ships took part in the invasion. Only two years later a similar force of Danes succeeded in overrunning England, which they would control until 1042.

The time had come for another of Brian's stratagems. In County Clare a wealth of folklore still surrounds Brian Boru. Folklore often embroiders an element of actual history. A story referring to the time of Brian's inauguration as high king is worth repeating here, because it illustrates a telling aspect of Brian's character. The Lia Fáil, or Stone of Destiny, still stands on the Hill of Tara, though today it stands upright. In an earlier age it lay flat on the earth. If a prospective Árd Rí stepped upon the stone and it shrieked aloud, that supposedly proved he was the true claimant to the office. It is said that in 1002 Brian Boru cleverly arranged for the Stone of Destiny to shriek aloud at just the right time. This mightily impressed the spectators, who declared him Árd Rí by acclamation.

In 1014 the night of 22 April was heavy with portents. Ravens screeched in the woodlands. Clouds roiled in a troubled sky. Gael and Viking alike cried out in their sleep, calling upon their God or their gods or their mothers. Later some of the Norsemen in Maelmora's army insisted that their god of war, the grim and implacable Woden, had ridden down the beach towards them in the dusk. He was mounted on a huge grey horse and wore an expression of unbearable grief. The effect this visitant had on the observers was almost paralytic.

There were omens for the Irish as well. One in particular stands out. Laiten, Brian's personal attendant, related that the Árd Rí had an unusual visitor on the eve of battle. Shortly after Laiten lit the king-candle at the entrance to Brian's tent, the banshee of the Dalcassians had appeared. Laiten related that he saw Ayvinn as clearly as if she were human: a pale, wraithlike woman, with long hair and a long face and a voice as soft as mist. What passed between them inside the tent was private and Brian did not share it with his servant. But after she left, the high king told Laiten that he and most of his sons would die on the morrow.

Laiten pleaded with him to refute the prophecy. Brian

only shook his head. He said he was too experienced to let himself be intimidated either by a supernatural visitant or by the numbers arrayed against him. The truth was simple: he was here and the enemy was there. The battle would be fought. If God was with them, then his army would win. Brian smiled his old, radiant smile to give the boy confidence. A confidence the Árd Rí may not have felt himself.

Ever since his days as king of Munster, Brian had made it his business to keep informed about events beyond the shores of Ireland. Therefore he knew that only the year before, a Danish king called Swein Forkbeard had sailed to the British mainland at the head of a massive invasion fleet. Thanks to their superior weapons his Vikings were defeating the native Britons, as well as the Anglians and Saxons who also were struggling for supremacy. His followers proclaimed Swein Forkbeard as king of a new Danish dominion.

Swein and his eldest son, Canute, planned to rule with an iron hand. The choicest lands were seized and occupied by the foreigners. New laws were promulgated. The old ways were swept away. The land which someday would be England, was coming under Danelaw.

Brian could not help comparing his situation with that of the hapless Britons. Sigurd the Stout and his allies had just brought a massive invasion fleet to Ireland. If the earl chose, he could sweep Maelmora and Sitric Silkbeard aside and make Ireland a Norse dominion.

Would God allow it? The children of Erin, unfree?

Not while I live.

Brave as he was, Brian Boru must have awaited the dawn with trepidation.

CHAPTER TEN

THE BATTLEGROUND

Clontarf – Cluain Tarbh in Irish – translates to 'The Meadow of the Bull'. The ancient name probably refers to the lush, watery meadows which lay above what is now Dollymount Strand. An alternative explanation for the name may come from the roar of the tide as it beats against the coastline, bellowing like a bull. The sandbank known as North Bull Island was not there at all in 1014, but there were several other small islands – including one called Clontarf. Placenames in early Ireland were always descriptive.

Although commemorated as 'the Battle of Clontarf', it would be more accurate to describe what happened in 1014 as 'the battle of the fishing-weir on the Tolka.' The Tolka River, which is approximately thirty kilometres in length, rises near Batterstown in County Meath. In 1014 the sea came much farther inland than it does today, and the Tolka, like the Liffey, was tidal.

There were several fishing weirs on the Tolka. The one nearest the mouth of the river was located some distance below what is now the Ballybough Bridge, and opposite the present-day Archbishop's House on the grounds of Holy Cross College. A thousand years ago the entire area was saturated twice daily by tidal inflow, which left the ground permanently waterlogged and useless for farming. But when the tide was out the weir was a good place for catching eels.

The Tolka discharged onto a broad expanse of sand known as the Furlong of Clontarf, approximately where Fairview Park is now. Clontarf Island, an offshore island formed, like modern Bull Island, by a natural accumulation of sand, was a prominent landmark. It was situated in deep water about 140 metres from the most easterly point of the present East Wall. The main low-tide channel of the Tolka lay between Clontarf Island and the shore.

From the summit of Howth, Sigurd the Stout could gaze with satisfaction on the many ships of his fleet. In the twilight even a sharp-eyed Viking could not make out the topography of the Irish mainland, but what Sigurd could see was enough to suit his purpose. The invasion force would have no difficulty going ashore in the morning; there were plenty of places to land their vessels.

It was all going to be so easy.

They would ride in on the dawn tide and disgorge the warriors fully armed and ready for battle. Judging by how long it took to load the ships, the last men probably would be going ashore about the time the battle was over. If the Irish high king was willing to fight at all. Good Friday. Sigurd licked his lips. The devout Gael might still be at their prayers when his men rolled over them like the waves of the sea.

Sigurd was impatient. He was always impatient – for food, for women, for treasure.

A wind was rising, bringing the smell of rain from the west. Stirring the black ashes of Fingal to life once more. There were streaks of crimson and gold in the distance, like brilliant lines etched on charcoal. Devils' eyes, winking and glaring. Sigurd glared back at them. Refusing to be frightened. Just one more day and all the land north of Dublin would be his. His men would extinguish the fires – or throw the Irish onto them.

According to Sitric Silkbeard, Brian's army was encamped somewhere west of the city. 'West of the city' meant nothing to the earl of Orkney. Just empty space.

More land that would soon be his after the obstacle of a feeble old man was eliminated. He could almost feel sorry for Brian Boru, but every man came to his swansong sooner or later. A Christian heaven or an Irish Valhalla would be waiting for the Árd Rí.

Gormlaith, the legend, was waiting for the earl of Orkney. With a sigh, Sigurd sought his bed for a few hours' sleep before the battle began.

In the palace in Dublin, Maelmora and Sitric Silkbeard were discussing the deployment of their troops in the morning. They would keep at it far into the night. Did Gormlaith hear them shouting as they argued? Knowing that he personally could stay safe behind the walls of Dublin, did her son insist on being designated as commander of the army?

Probably not. Maelmora would not have allowed it. The king of Leinster had many faults, but only once in his life had he been accused of cowardice. In the battle to come he meant to expiate the shame of Glenmama once and for all. When their combined forces marched out in the morning he was determined to lead them to victory.

From this point on it will be less confusing to designate the opposing forces as 'the Irish' and 'the foreigners', which is how it was done by the annalists of the time.

Bear in mind that these labels are woefully inaccurate. The men on both sides who would fight to the death on Good Friday represented almost every country in Western Europe. Some would be fighting for home and tribe, others for land and riches, still others simply because they followed a certain banner.

In the end they would be equally dead.

The Irish were up and moving long before dawn. On the previous night Brian had given specific orders which were to be followed before the first foreigners came ashore. His sons and commanders were obeying his plan to the letter. Only the Árd Rí himself was exempt from the action. While his warriors moved swiftly, silently, through field and forest to take up their pre-ordained positions, Brian accompanied his personal attendant and his bodyguards to the site he had selected for his tent.

Not a command post, not this time. The command would be Murrough's, beneath the blue banner of the Dál gCais. Brian would wait in relative obscurity; wait with dry mouth and pounding heart for the first news from the front lines of the battle. Because he was determined that the enemy be confined to a specific area north of Dublin and not permitted to infiltrate the countryside and collect allies, he had chosen the battleground in advance, and with his usual care.

Until the introduction of long-range artillery and air power, the physical layout of a battlefield was crucial. The deeds of Good Friday, 1014, would be told and re-told, the carefully memorised names of the heroes endlessly recited, but no chroniclers specified the exact locations of certain episodes. In the beginning it must have been assumed that the listeners were familiar enough with the locale. But sadly, when the last survivor of the battle finally died, his knowledge died with him. Apparently what the combatants knew of the ground on which they fought was never passed on.

As a result there has long been a difference of opinion as to where Brian's tent was pitched. Half a dozen locations have been mooted, just as several possibilities for the main battlefield have been named.

But physical evidence tells the story. In 1014 there were two elevations – two outstanding points of high ground – north of the walled city of Dublin and the River Liffey. One was around present-day Mountjoy Square. The other was a height to the west of this, called Magh Dumha, much of which was covered by a dense forest of ancient oaks, holly and arbutus known as Tomar's Wood. In modern north Dublin that area comprises part of Phibsborough.

The Magh Dumha location is preferred by those who believe Brian's tent was placed directly in front of Tomar's Wood. Before the day was over Tomar's Wood would become infamous, which may be the reason it was vividly remembered. What happened there would long linger in the mind. However, it may not have involved Brian Boru.

If the Árd Rí's tent had been set up at Magh Dumha the opaque expanse of Tomar's Wood would have blocked his line of sight in the direction of his encampment – and a possible retreat. As a wise general, Brian had always kept his retreats open. Tomar's Wood was also the perfect place for an ambush, making the location far too dangerous for a non-combatant high king.

A thorough topographical examination of the entire area reveals that in 1014 the only unimpeded view in all directions, including the critical Tolka valley, would have been from a plateau directly north of the city and closer to the bay. Since the late eighteenth century that plateau has been crowned by Mountjoy Square.

On the high ground – it must always be the high ground – his men erected the tent of the Árd Rí, a small pavilion of leather and linen, furnished with sparse but kingly appointments. A wealth of cushions for an old man to rest upon, a carved prayer stool for his devotions. The tent was placed within a stand of saplings, and screens covered with the untanned hide of brindle cows were arranged to provide additional camouflage. Brian's bodyguards were satisfied that the location was well concealed while meeting the high king's requirements. Brian had demanded a vantage point from which he could see the entire field of battle once dawn came. From the shelter of the trees a few steps in any direction would offer an excellent view. The position would be far in advance of his lines but Brian had always gone ahead. He saw no reason to break the habit of a lifetime.

We do not know if Laiten lit the king-candle in front of the Árd Rí's tent, but it is unlikely. The light would have attracted too much attention. Brian probably did have a small bronze lamp which was safe to use inside the tent. A king must never be left in the dark.

As he waited for the dawn, Brian envisioned the day to come. He had made it his business to learn this land; he knew the cattle tracks and boggy pools, knew where vision was hampered by a fold in the earth, where a stony outcropping offered the opportunity for an ambush, where a stretch of open ground made a frontal attack possible, where he ... where Murrough ... might need to deploy extra troops.

While the last stars faded Brian watched the battle unfold in his mind. Step by step, like a chess game. A bad omen, he warned himself, that image of a chess game. Brian shrugged off the thought. He had lived a long life and used himself totally. There were scars on his body that only his personal servants saw, and scars on his soul that only his God saw.

Brian Boru ordered Laiten to unfold his personal prayer stool and set it up in his tent. As was his lifelong habit, Brian then unsheathed his sword and placed it within easy reach.

The Leinstermen and the Danes of Dublin were in motion too. Scouts reported that some of Brian's troops had been observed taking up positions to the north. In eager anticipation, several thousand warriors speaking a variety of local dialects crowded around the walls of the city, spreading out along the tidal mud flats, elbowing one another in the dark. The sound of their shuffling feet was like the roar of a storm wind.

Maelmora insisted on marching out of Dublin at the head of both armies, as if they and the city were his own. He was determined to be given credit for the victory to come. Let the northern auxiliaries plug the holes and chase down the deserters. This time the glory would go to Leinster!

Maelmora's claim of precedence was vigorously rejected by a Danish prince known as Dubhgall, who may have been another son of Olaf Cuaran and thus was a half-brother to Sitric Silkbeard. As the armies began to move the two men struck up a quarrel that would not end that day, not until both were dead.

Sigurd and Brodir, who were more accustomed to fighting from the sea rather than on the land, gave little thought to the physical terrain of the battle, but they fully appreciated the importance of having an overwhelming number of warriors at their disposal. All that mattered was getting in first with the most savage offence. A terrifying beginning was what successful warfare required – frighten the other side so badly their senses deserted them and they could not think, only run. Then chase them down, kill them, and claim the spoils.

The Vikings were ready. They bared their teeth at one another, practising their most savage grins.

Meanwhile Brian's warriors hastened to take up the positions assigned to them. It was not easy in the dark but they had no choice: the Árd Rí's instructions to his commanders had been explicit. Moving as stealthily as possible, they had crossed the Liffey at several points during the night, including the old Hurdle Ford. So many trampling feet must have totally destroyed the hurdles.

Upon reaching the north shore, the three Irish battalions and their Norse allies angled across what is now the Phoenix Park and moved out onto the fields north of the city, where they began to disperse in a broad front facing the bay. At this point Malachy Mór and his warriors may have come from their encampment and rejoined Brian's men, but there has long been controversy over this issue.

Cogadh Gaedhel re Gallaibh states that Malachy had made a deal with the foreigners in advance to 'put a ditch between him and the foreigners; and that if he would not attack the foreigners, they would not attack him.' The claim cannot be proved or disproved, but this account had been commissioned by Brian Boru's great-grandson and was undoubtedly partisan.

Malachy's partisans always claimed that the former high king took part in the battle and fought heroically. Yet his deeds on the battlefield of Clontarf are not recounted in any of the annals. More tellingly, no prince of Meath was named in the extensive lists of casualties. Malachy's Meathmen had been invited to fight beside the warriors of Thomond, but their presence among the Dalcassians is not reported. If the battalion from Meath had joined in the battle from the beginning and managed to get through that terrible day unscathed, it was a miracle of biblical proportions.

Possibly Malachy and his warriors waited on the high ground around Magh Dumha. They might have used the oak forest for cover until they decided which way the battle was going, then hurried forward to be on the winning side. The truth of the matter probably will never be known, but we can be reasonably confident that Malachy Mór was present that day. He was the only prince of the Gael who survived to leave an eyewitness account.

Of Brian's army, the annalists wrote: 'They had with them an abundance of steel; strong, piercing, graceful, ornamental, smooth, sharp pointed, bright sided, keen, clean, glittering, flashing, well-tempered, quick, sharp swords, in the beautiful white hands of chiefs and royal knights, for hewing and for hacking, for maiming and mutilating skins and bodies and skulls.'

Like the Norse, the Gael loved the drama of warfare and saw beauty in the tools of butchery. Unfortunately for them, their tools of butchery were, for the most part, inferior to those of the Northmen. Only one weapon made them equal. Brian had taught his men to use the Viking battle axe.

His army was as prepared as it could possibly be. There was nothing left to be done now, but stand and fight.

It would not be logical to assume that a man who

had built his entire career upon strategic planning, clever tactics, and doing the unexpected, would, in the final great battle of his life, rely on the old reckless, headlong attack that left so much to chance. Brian left nothing to chance. An examination of the principal battleground, even today, tells the story.

No modern observer can see the terrain which Brian saw. Today it comprises north Dublin and is covered with buildings and streets and people. The shape of the land itself has been altered; much of it has been eaten away by flood or piled high by bulldozers. Yet underneath remains the soil which was soaked with blood on that Good Friday. The main elements upon which Brian predicated victory are still there too.

The Árd Rí had decided the Irish should make their stand between the Liffey and the Tolka rivers, an area bounded on the north by impenetrable forest and on the south by the marshy lowlands of Clontarf, and the sea. Brian wanted his army to be clearly visible to the invaders as they came ashore. Luring them to fight on his selected battleground.

Do any reliably accepted documents exist to prove this? No. But subsequent events bear it out.

In the dark that preceded dawn, gooseflesh rose on the arms of brave men. It was not the cold that affected them, or the knowledge of possible death. In that brief space of time they were trapped as if in a bubble, aware of all the possibilities and yet untouched by them. The battle was still theirs to win.

It is a thrilling experience to which a warrior may become addicted. If he survives.

• • • • • • • • •

CHAPTER ELEVEN

Battle Morning
Sunrise, 23 April 1014

The first golden rays pierced the ranks of dark cloud hanging over the Irish Sea.

In the city of Dublin women awoke beside their snoring husbands and reluctantly left their beds to rake the coals on the hearth and relight the cooking fires. Twists of cloth were thrust into lamps filled with rancid fat and set alight. Buckets brimming with night soil were thrown out into the road. The morning meal would be the same as that of the night before: boiled pottage and black bread and pickled herrings. Perhaps, considering what the day might bring, a good wife might produce a bit of roast meat she had been saving and offer it to her man, along with a bowl of soured milk. He might be going out to die.

Throughout the Irish countryside women awoke and left their beds to rake the coals and relight the fires. They had the same duties, the same worries, as their sisters in the city. The food they prepared was different, as was the language they spoke, but they all felt the cold of early morning. Those whose husbands had marched off to battle might be murmuring prayers for their safety.

Christian women in Dublin might be praying too for God to protect their men that day.

North of the River Liffey, the battalions of thrushes and warblers and blackbirds who serenaded the dawn to mark out their territories grew quiet. This was not a day for singing. The armies of gulls and terns and guillemots who fed greedily along the shore of the bay abandoned their breakfasts and fled into the sky. It was not yet time for screaming.

But the time was coming. In the unnatural silence which descended, all were aware that something momentous was about to happen.

The Vikings began landing at high tide. From his position Brian could see the foreigners climbing out of their longships and splashing through the shallows. Some of those vessels could carry from eighty to a hundred men, but Brian did not try to calculate the number of invaders. It did not matter. All that mattered was the courage of his own men and how well they followed orders.

As the Vikings went ashore Maelmora of Leinster hurried forward to make his presence known to their leaders. If he had hoped to be put in charge of the foreign forces he was disappointed; Sigurd and Brodir had no intention of relinquishing any of their command, even to each other. Sigurd was wrong if he had thought Brian might not fight him. Maelmora pointed out that the Irish already were taking up positions. Over that way; see them? In plain sight! There was no time to waste; the Irish were forcing the battle. They must be attacked at once!

For once, Sigurd and Brodir agreed with him. The Viking warriors prepared for what would prove to be a very long day. The ships that delivered them to the flooded foreshore between the Liffey and the Tolka hastily withdrew to a point well beyond Clontarf Island in order to avoid being trapped by the tide, which was already falling.

The Irish battle line was widely spaced, stretching almost from river to river. They would begin the fight with their backs to the land, the foreigners with their backs to the sea. Over the intervening centuries a number of reconstructions of the deployment of troops on both sides have been offered. In the manner beloved by writers of antiquity these are replete with long lists of the combatants, some of whom could not possibly have been at Clontarf – nor even alive at the time. None of these creations can be accepted as accurate history.

The consensus amongst scholars is that Murrough and his Dalcassians began the battle in the centre of the Irish line, or alternatively on the Irish left, near the valley of the Tolka. Supporting them were the rest of the men of Thomond under the command of Brian's sons, Flann and Conor. Other officers in this division included the prince of Corca Bhaiscinn and a lord of the Déisi from Waterford.

The second division of the Irish contained the warriors of south Munster, including the Owenachts and their allied tribes. The third division was built around the Connachtmen, led by Tadhg, king of the Uí Maine, and the princes of the west. This battalion was supported by the noble Scots – the ancestors of the royal Stewarts and the Gael of Alba would fight for Ireland that day.

There is no trustworthy description of the disposition of the foreigners' troops. After some arguing, no doubt, the command may have been a triumvirate consisting of Sigurd, Brodir and Maelmora. Like the Irish, their forces were composed of three divisions. One consisted of the Danes of Dublin, led by Dubhgall Olaffson and augmented by a band of foreign auxiliaries under the command of four Viking princes. The battalion containing the majority of the foreigners was commanded by the earl of Orkney. At Maelmora's insistence, the third division was built around his Leinstermen and their Norse allies from southeast Ireland.

The chroniclers are not clear about which group was awarded the presence of Brodir. But they agree on one point: led by Sigurd's ally, the savage Norse warrior called Anrud, the thousand mercenaries in chainmail hauberks were at the very forefront when the battle began. These constituted the eleventh-century equivalent of a weapon of mass destruction, terrifying in their appearance and lethal in their capabilities.

Responding to the line created by the Irish and their Norse allies, this army of the foreigners, with its strongly Irish component, stretched out across the open fields, facing their opponents. In some places their line was three men deep.

Initially an empty no-man's land yawned between the two armies. They could see each other, hate each other. But the moment was not yet upon them.

Amongst the Irish there was one exception to the

traditional style of warfare. In a sparsely populated land it was important to spare as many lives as possible, particularly those of healthy men of breeding age. Since the era of Cúchulainn, the Gael had observed the Combat of Champions. When opposing forces faced one another and before battle was joined, the leader of one side might ask for a Combat of Champions. If the other side agreed, the two best warriors were sent out to fight to the death. The man left still standing not only won the contest, but won the battle for his side. The two armies could then retire in honour from the field with only one casualty between them.

This highly stylised custom depended on each side having a legitimate champion, a man whose individual fighting prowess was famous. To offer a lesser warrior was to insult the other side and would be rejected. As a result, the Combat of Champions was something of a rarity. In his day Brian Boru had participated in a number of them. It is claimed that when he was seventy-two years old he fought his last such combat and won it, perhaps with the discreet assistance of a trusted shield bearer.

The Árd Rí would not take part in a Combat of Champions that morning. Above all else, Brian was a realist. He knew the effort was beyond him now, even if the other side were willing. They would not be; the purpose of the invasion was clear. Nothing would satisfy Sitric and Maelmora but the destruction of the high king's armies and the death of Brian himself.

In addition to his own son Murrough, Brian Boru had two outstanding champions following his banner: they were the Great Steward of Marr and the Great Steward of Lennox. According to one version of the battle, Donald of Marr came forward to the space between the lines and called for a champion from the other side to meet him. A Viking named Platt stepped forward to take up the challenge. As the story goes, they fought in plain sight of the two armies until both men fell dead, each with his sword through the heart of the other.

Whether this episode actually happened or not, nothing could prevent the battle which followed. It had its own impetus, propelled by anger and ambition in equal measure. The Irish line advanced. The foreigners marched forward to meet them. The very air between the two vast armies shivered with tension.

There was enough light now for at least part of the battlefield to be visible to anyone watching from the city, and many were. Sitric Silkbeard and his entourage had ensconced themselves on the wooden walkway just inside the palisades. From this vantage point they could see some of Dublin Bay and some of the ground to the north of the Liffey. Confident of victory, at first Sitric may have played the role of a host at a sporting event, calling for goblets of beer for his guests and laying wagers as to how soon the Irish would surrender. But wagering was premature.

To the onlookers on the palisades the event may have seemed very slow to start. There was a lot of shouting and a lot of manoeuvring. Much of what happened was not visible to the Dubliners at all, but for sheer excitement the possibilities would be hard to match.

They were not able to see what Brian Boru saw as he stood outside his tent. Leaning, perhaps, on the strong shoulder of young Laiten, and impatiently ordering his bodyguards to step out of the way and not block his view. The captain of those bodyguards was Niall Ua Cuinn, a Dalcassian with an exceptional reputation as a warrior. His was the honour of being Brian's personal protector, the man who would take any sword thrust meant for the Árd Rí. To his regret, the son of Quinn had never been called upon to give his life for his king. Neither had his father, the man who had held the post before him.

As Niall watched with Brian and the others, Murrough suddenly strode forward alone except for the man who carried his blue banner. Facing the enemy, Brian's son drew himself to his full height and brandished his sword in defiance.

His heroism made a profound impression on all who saw it. Even the foreigners did not react, but stared in admiration.

Brian gave a cry of alarm. He ordered one of his bodyguards to run to Murrough at once and tell him he must return to his troops immediately; it was imperative that he live to lead the army. The man ran faster than he ever had in his life. When he told Murrough that his father commanded him to withdraw, the prince looked as if he did not understand; he was like a man waking from a dream. Abruptly, he turned on his heel and returned to the Dalcassians.

But the signal had been given. The battle began.

CHAPTER TWELVE

ATTACK!

The first-century Greek geographer and historian Strabo had written of the Celts: 'The whole race is madly fond of war, high-spirited and quick to battle, and on whatever pretext you stir them up you will find them ready to face danger, even if they have nothing on their side but their own strength and courage.' A thousand years later this was equally applicable to their Irish descendants.

The Gael and the Northmen had raw courage in common, and also their traditional method of attack. Warriors on both sides began by making menacing gestures and screaming insults at one another until their blood was sufficiently heated, then charged forward on a broad front, smashing their way into their opponents.

The side that did the most damage and broke the other's nerve usually won.

Warfare would continue to be conducted in a more or less similar fashion until the twentieth century. The horrors of World War One, when hundreds of thousands of doomed soldiers were sent 'over the top' to certain death, had a profound effect on future combat.

In 1014 tribalism determined the composition of the Irish divisions. The noble lords of the Gael commanded their personal armies of warriors within the ranks of their battalions. But once the battle began, another factor took over. Princes and kings on both sides were easily identified by their banners. The leaders of the two great armies began deliberately targeting one another, as if in a Combat of Champions. Military cohesion began to break down.

Cogadh Gaedhel re Gallaibh offers the following lurid impression of the opening moments of the Battle of Clontarf: 'There arose a wild, impetuous, precipitate, furious, dark, frightful, voracious, merciless, combative, contentious, vulture-like screaming and fluttering over their heads. And there arose also the satyrs, and the idiots, and the maniacs of the valleys, and the witches, and the goblins, and the ancient birds, and the destroying demons of the air and of the firmament, and the feeble demoniac phantom host; and they were screaming and comparing the valour and combat of both parties.'

Beneath this wildly extravagant narrative lies a kernel of truth. The most epic of all Irish battles was horrendous in the extreme. Hand-to-hand combat with bladed weapons is physically exhausting. Cinema and television to the contrary, people do not automatically lie down and die when someone sticks a sword into them. The human hide is surprisingly tough. Considerable force is required to drive a blade into a person, and it is almost as difficult to pull it out. Even then your enemy may get to his feet and come at you again. The recently discovered skeleton of Richard III, the last Plantagenet king of England, reveals that he suffered a score of incredibly savage wounds before finally succumbing to a fractured skull.

Early in the day, the men of Connacht confronted the Danes of Dublin. A savage battle took place between them in which most of the combatants were killed. Of the Connachtmen, less than a hundred survived. With them died Murray, the Great Steward of Lennox. The Danes of Dublin lost all but twenty of their number. The valiant Dubhgall attempted to take the survivors to join another battalion, but his own survival would be brief. He was slain at the foot of the bridge which was afterwards given his name.

Anrud and his battalion in chainmail smashed full force into the Dalcassians, hacking and slashing their way amongst them. In that terrible onrush Murrough's men fell back at first, but their leader stood firm as the blood began to spray around him. Swinging a sword in either hand – apparently he was one of the few Gaels to possess equal dexterity, striking left or right – Murrough charged headlong into the armoured battalion. Iron met iron and steel met steel. His men followed him. The weapons of the Dalcassians came to life with a mighty clashing against the thrice-riveted armour of their adversaries.

The observers watching from the battlements of Dublin claimed afterwards that they could see flashes of fire in the air all around the warriors.

They were surging back and forth across the uneven ground, up and down the hillocks, through the thickets, around the boulders, fighting every step of the way. There would be no pauses to catch one's breath and no stop for a rest. When a warrior fell a replacement did not always hurry forward to fight in his stead; and even if one did, he would have to step over his predecessor's body. If a man grew desperately thirsty – and fighting was thirsty work – he might be lucky enough to come upon a brook, or a spring, or some farmer's well where he might slake his thirst, but that moment of inattention could easily earn him a spear in the back.

Whatever moments of glory the combatants originally had imagined soon turned into physical anguish and agonising pain. There was no one available to tend the wounded. Not even a priest to pray over them. Nothing but the imperative to kill.

Murrough's actions that morning were described by the chroniclers as 'the fierce rushing of a bull, and the scorching path of a royal champion'. He was said to be the last man in Erin who was a match for a hundred. Against the odds, he and his Dalcassians finally hacked the armoured mercenaries to pieces. This unexpected turn of events so shocked Anrud that he ran amok across the fields, mindlessly dodging the spears thrown at him. The Irish annalists would call Brian Boru's oldest son 'the gate of battle, the hurdle of conflict, the sheltering tree and the impregnable tower'.

Those annalists, who were so effusive in their praise of the Gael, were not stinting in their praise of the foreigners. It was the Irish tradition for a man to respect the foe he defeated, rather than denigrating him. There was no glory in defeating a mediocrity. Consider the following: 'The terrible swords maimed and cut the comely, graceful bodies of noble, pleasant, courteous, affable, accomplished men on both sides. There was the clashing of two bodies of equal hardness, and of two bodies moving in contrary directions, in one place. And it is not easy to imagine what to liken it to; but to nothing small could be likened the firm, stern, sudden, thunder-motion; and the stout, haughty billow-roll of these people on both sides.'

In literature there are two views of the Battle of Clontarf, one presented by the Irish annalists and the other by the Norse sagas. The Irish rely on spectacular overstatement for their effect. The Norse rely on tight-lipped understatement. There is one noteworthy exception to this. Old Norse poetry includes 'The Song of the Valkyries' which prophesies the carnage of Clontarf. Gleaming with a dark and terrible splendour, it describes a crimson dawn painted by the blood of warriors as the battle maidens with flying hair ride forth on their wild horses, eager to claim the fallen heroes.

In the fields above the Irish Sea the warriors fought man to man and breast to breast, one grimacing face glaring into another. Those on one side who made a kill soon fell victim to someone from the other side. Battle-crazed warriors began taking trophy heads, in the style of the ancient Celts.

The conflict took on a life of its own. Seen from above it would have resembled a giant sprawling multicoloured beast clawing its way over the rolling land, a creature with a broken back, perhaps, that twitched and spasmed, briefly revealing the dark gleam of metal scales along its sides.

Yet all was not as chaotic as it appeared, not at first. Brian had studied classical warfare. Through the chain of command, the few trusted princes to whom the Árd Rí had confided the full details of his battle plan passed the necessary information on to the ranking officers below them. These men were responsible for organising the warriors in the field. The ordinary foot soldier did not need to know the whole picture. All that was required was that he obey the commands of his immediate leader.

Sigurd the Stout had been wrong in his assessment of the battle. It was not quickly over. The Irish did not yield but they moved back slowly, one step at a time, giving away each foot of ground with the greatest reluctance. Forcing the foreigners to come after them.

The tide of battle flowed first one way, then another, but always and ultimately towards Magh Dumha on the heights, where stood Tomar's Wood.

Although the main action took place on the battleground Brian had chosen, there was sporadic fighting elsewhere as well. In the rush to come ashore, several of the Viking ships had made landfall farther along the coast. Bones and remnants of weapons dated to this time have been found at Fairview, in an area of Marino known until recently as 'the Bloody Fields', and on the strand of Sandymount below the walls of Dublin. For several hours tardy foreigners rushed to join their comrades.

Brian's army had no reinforcements on the way. Every warrior the men of Erin could gather was already fully committed. Or should have been.

Through what became an interminable day the inhabitants of Dublin, including Sitric Silkbeard and his wife and mother, watched the fighting from the palisades along the Liffey. They could not see all of the action, or even the climactic moments, but they witnessed a panorama of fighting and killing sufficient to satisfy the most bloodthirsty observer. A chronicler relates, 'The men and women who were watching from the battlements of Áth Cliath saw flashes of fire' – the sun glinting off helmets and blades.

Swinging and slashing and cutting and chopping. Screams of fury; cries of agony. And still the battle went on.

According to Sitric Silkbeard, 'not more numerous would be the sheaves floating over a great company reaping a field of oats than was the hair flying with the wind, cut away by heavy gleaming axes and by bright flaming swords.' He supposedly remarked to his wife, Brian

Boru's daughter, 'Well do the foreigners reap the field; many is the sheaf they let go from them.' Emer is said to have replied, 'It will be at the end of the day that will be seen.'

The fiercest fighting took place in the centre of the battlefield. In the only statement of his which survives, Malachy Mór is reputed to have said, 'I never saw a battle like it, nor have I heard of its equal. There was a field and a ditch between us and them, and the sharp wind of the spring coming over them towards us. In not more than the time it would take to milk two cows, not one person could recognise another, though it might be his son or his brother that was nearest him, unless he should know his voice. We were so covered, as well our heads as our faces, with the drops of gory blood, carried by the force of the sharp cold wind which passed over them to us. And even if we attempted to perform any deed of valour we were unable to do it, because our spears over our heads had become clogged and bound with long locks of hair which the wind forced upon us, so it was half occupation with us to endeavour to disentangle and cast them off. And it is one of the problems of Erin, whether the valour of those who sustained that crushing assault was greater than ours who bore the sight of it without running distracted before the winds or fainting.'

Again and again Brian Boru said to his attendant, 'Your eyes are younger and sharper than mine, Laiten. Can you still see the standard of Prince Murrough?' And Laiten replied, 'I can indeed, lord; he is hewing his way across the battlefield with the enemy falling to the right and the left of him.' Satisfied for a time, the old man knelt on his cushioned prayer stool and folded his hands.

Laiten did not tell the Árd Rí when he saw Flann's banner go down, nor when Conor's banner disappeared beneath the trampling feet of the foreigners. Brian probably did not ask. He knew too well the nature of battle.

Men died by the hundreds; then by the thousands. Maelmora, king of Leinster, was slain by Brian's nephew Conaing, he of the ill-fated chess match at Kincora. The enmity between them lasted to the end; before he fell lifeless, Maelmora inflicted a fatal wound on Conaing.

The sun passed its high point and began to slip towards the west. In the confusion of battle nothing seemed certain. Slowly Brian's army continued to fall back. Inland, upland, away from the sea.

Brodir was wading through the ranks of the Irish and wreaking havoc with his axe. *Njal's Saga,* which was originally written in Old Norse, tells us what happened next from the Viking point of view. An Irish prince whom the Norse identify as 'Ulf Hreda' challenged Brodir and 'thrust at him thrice, so hard that Brodir could hardly regain his feet.' Obviously he was badly shaken. As soon as he succeeded in getting up he fled to the nearest patch of woods.

The leaders of both sides were dying in large numbers now. Chieftains and kings, marked out by one another, lay on the ground in their own blood.

Some time during this long day Murrough confronted Sigurd the Stout. He broke through the ranks of foreigners surrounding the earl of Orkney and ran up to the highly conspicuous raven banner. Murrough promptly killed the man carrying the banner. Sigurd ordered another man to take up his standard immediately. He did, and Murrough killed him too. A furious battle then ensued between Brian's son and Sigurd's followers, but they were reluctant to get close enough to kill him.

According to *Njal's Saga*, Earl Sigurd ordered Thorstein Hallsson to lift his banner from the ground. He was about to obey when Amundi the White called out, 'Don't take the banner, Thorstein! All who bear it will be slain!'

Earl Sigurd cried, 'Hrafn the Red, you carry my banner!'

The intrepid Hrafn replied, 'Carry it yourself.'

Sigurd did not lack in courage. He reputedly remarked, 'Likely it is most fitting that bag and beggar stay together.'

He tore the raven banner from its staff and tucked it into his belt. Then he turned to Murrough and attacked him, but the Irishman was quicker. He struck off Sigurd's helmet with a single blow of the sword in his right hand, bursting both strap and buckles. With his left hand Murrough struck again. As he fell, the earl of Orkney wrapped the raven banner around himself. The raven became his winding sheet.

It took half of the afternoon for the foreigners to force the Irish as far as Tomar's Wood. There Brian's army made its stand, refusing to be driven any farther. The foreigners pursued them with their axes. The Irish retaliated with theirs.

Normal emotion was transformed into a boiling eruption of fear and hate, shared by both sides. What happened then was a living nightmare that would haunt the men who experienced it for the rest of their lives. They were afraid to close their eyes in sleep for fear they would see it again – see and hear and smell it all again.

According to Malachy Mór's poet and historian, Mac Coisse, 'in Tomar's Wood where the fiercest of the axe fighting took place, blood was still dripping from the trees three days later.'

One historian claims that the Irish chopped down trees in Tomar's Wood to use for building fires. This is implausible. Their enemies would never have granted them time out for lighting fires and cooking meals.

Yet amidst all the horrors of the daylong battle there were individual moments of grace and mercy. Murrough or one of his men came across Thorstein trying to rebind the thongs that held his shoes to his feet. When the Irishman asked why he had paused for so mundane a task, Thorstein sadly replied, 'Because I shall not get home to Iceland tonight.' The Irishman sheathed his sword and let him live.

Another of the Irish warriors who was forced by nature to empty his bowels was discovered by one of the Danes, who promptly crouched down and joined him. After sharing this moment of extreme vulnerability, the two went their separate ways.

A small child wandered onto the outermost edge of the battlefield, searching for firewood. Men from both sides rushed forward to head him off and lead him to a place of safety.

And still the killing went on.

There is nothing to compare with the appalling, unmistakeable din of battle. The screams and curses and clash of metal on metal. No officer could shout loudly enough to be certain his order were heard. Veterans fought in savage silence, knowing that every breath was valuable and might be the last.

In the crowded loneliness of battle, before the ultimate loneliness of dying, a man sought affirmation of his own life.

Men who have died in battle are rarely good to look upon. No matter how splendid their appearance at the apex of heroism, when the soul has fled it takes all grace and beauty with it. Bowels empty, mouths gape, bellies swell, dead eyes gleam fishbelly white. Nothing visible remains of glory. In the tents of death all men belong to the same tribe.

Late in the afternoon, perhaps around four o'clock, the last surviving Irish commanders issued what would be their final order to their men: Go back the way you came. Go down from the high ground at Magh Dumha towards the valley of the Tolka. And the sea.

CHAPTER THIRTEEN

THE END OF THE DAY

Trampled mud and blood-soaked grass made the ground so slippery it was hard to keep one's feet. The Irish warriors struggled to obey the commands they were given. Most of their princes and chieftains were dead or dying by now, but at least they still had Murrough's standard to follow. What remained of Brian's army turned and headed back down the battlefield. Exhausted men, covered with blood, their own and that of other men.

The battle which had begun with the sunrise would last until sunset, but its nature changed. The Viking fury which had sustained the foreigners for so long was fading fast. They knew in their bones that they were defeated; they remembered the ancient axiom, 'Men who never quit cannot lose.'

Brian's army would never quit. Following Murrough's brilliant blue banner, the flag of the Dalcassians, they drove their enemies across the fields in the direction of the valley of the Tolka. Slashing, hacking, a snarl of men fighting every step of the way, without any order but with deadly determination. They too realised they were going to win.

Perhaps this was the moment when Malachy Mór decided to join the battle. He unquestionably entered the fray at some point, because he was there at the end. Malachy has always had his partisans. In his book *The History of Ireland to the Coming of Henry the II,* Arthur Ua Clerigh even gives Malachy credit for the victory of Clontarf.

The Irish accounts of the battle which have come down to us through the annals had been related by the survivors to their children and grandchildren. The survivors were ordinary foot soldiers, who went where they were told without asking why. Every high-ranking commander who executed the orders personally given by Brian Boru in that final meeting died on Good Friday. This is a crucial point that has long been ignored. What those men knew about Brian's specific battle plans would never be told.

A telling passage in *Cogadh Gaedhel re Gallaibh* states, 'The full events of that battle and its deeds God alone knows, because every one who could have knowledge of it fell there on either side.'

Hand-to-hand battles are chaotic. They seem to have no plan and follow no design, other than kill or be killed. A warrior must trust his leader to know what is going on. For the man in the midst of it all and fighting for his life, there is nothing but noise and confusion. Therefore this was the scene the survivors of Clontarf described. For a thousand years, people studying the battle have accepted this as the complete story and overlooked the one factor that made all the difference. The mind of Brian Boru.

On different occasions Brian had spent considerable time in and around Dublin; at the end of 999 he was there for months. Obviously he had explored the locale in detail, as was his habit. Following his orders, his men had dismantled fortresses and cleared strategic passes in a wide area around the city and its approaches. The chronicles agree on this point. With a keen eye for observation and an intuitive sense of tactical possibilities, Brian would have, consciously or subconsciously, rehearsed for what was to come.

Like many another great general, including Robert the Bruce at the Battle of Bannockburn, Brian Boru chose the terrain at Clontarf and dictated the terms by which the battle would be fought. He may have hoped to forestall events until after Easter, but if he waited any longer the invaders would come much farther inland. His army would have faced the enemy on different ground, and that would have spoiled everything.

Brian knew more than the lie of the land; during an earlier reconnoitring he must have taken time to study the effect of the tides. The high spring tide that delivered the foreigners in the morning had fallen back by midday. The ships which brought them had withdrawn so they would not be trapped by the receding waters. The few men left aboard may not have realised what was happening to their forces on land until it was too late.

The Árd Rí's chosen battleground was relatively narrow, uneven, and bounded by tidal rivers on both sides, with an impenetrable forest at the top and the sea at the bottom. In flood tide the pleasant little fishing-river of the Tolka became something else entirely. Until very recent times it was a source of major flooding in north Dublin, finally tamed at considerable expense by cement walls and determined engineers.

By late afternoon the weir of Clontarf was completely under water. Darkly roiling, seething, foam-crested sea-water that carried all before it. The valley of the Tolka was flooded almost as far as where the Botanic Gardens bloom today. The appalled Vikings in the forefront of the retreat must have realised they could not hope to reach their ships. A vast expanse of turbulent water from Dublin Bay lay between them and safety.

The Irish were upon them now. When they realised the foreigners were trying to get away, Brian's army attacked the enemy with all the savagery they themselves had received.

On the twenty-third of April, 1014, the valley of the Tolka became a killing field.

Caught by the surging water, the foreigners fought for their lives. As soon as a man crawled out of the flood he was cut down by sword and axe – or even bashed in the head with a mace. The warriors of the Irish army stalked the edge of the water like predators seeking their prey. The Tolka River ran red.

After the tide receded the body of Brian's grandson Turlough, would be found in the riverbed. His two strong young hands were still clutching the yellow hair of a dead invader. (According to ambulance drivers in north Dublin today, one remaining deep pool of the Tolka below Ballybough Bridge has an irresistible attraction to would-be suicides.)

A few surviving Danes who were unwilling or unable to flee fought for their lives in the open fields. The Irish pursued them there too. When the shadows grew long with the approach of evening, Murrough's arms were so weary he could barely lift them. His faithful shield bearer had long since fallen. He could no longer manage both his shield and his sword, so he let the shield go. Moments later he was attacked by the crazed chieftain, Anrud.

Murrough reportedly closed with him, seizing the Norseman with his left hand and pulling off the man's hauberk with his right. With an effort he flung his foe to the ground. He drove his sword into Anrud's prostrate body by pressing on it with all his weight. But he was too tired; his reflexes had become too slow. When Anrud reached up with a dying effort and pulled Murrough's dagger from its scabbard he did not even notice. The dagger sank deep into Murrough's side. It would be a mortal wound.

This time when Brian asked if Laiten could see Murrough's banner, the young man closed his eyes and shook his head.

Suddenly the Árd Rí's tent must have seemed very dark. And very cold.

Murrough would live until the following morning, long enough to make his confession and receive the Sacrament. Then Brian's heir, the man who best knew his father's plans and shared his vision, died.

Before darkness fell on that grim Good Friday, the

remaining Leinstermen made the mistake of fleeing to the city for safety. They made for Dubhgall's Bridge, where they were met by the Liffey in full flood. By now a few of the Viking longships, aware of their plight, were moving towards the city, but they could not be reached by the terrified warriors because the whole area around Dubhgall's Bridge was under water.

Once again the tide was flowing over the sands of Dublin Bay, but not in the bright light of dawn. The light was lurid now – ghastly. The setting sun turned the sky to crimson. The blood of the invaders turned the water to crimson.

The watchers on the palisades of Dublin were aghast – except for Emer, Brian Boru's daughter. According to the chronicles, she could not resist crowing: 'It appears to me that the foreigners have gained their inheritance.' When Sitric Silkbeard asked what she meant, she replied, 'The foreigners are going into the sea, their natural inheritance.' Sitric was so angry he hit her in the mouth with his fist.

The last of the fighting was the most bitter. Men who knew they had nothing to lose but their life, and no longer cared about that, demonstrated the savagery that could lurk beneath supposedly civilised skin. When there was no hope left, there was only death and they embraced it with fury. The Christians who had followed the banners of the Dalcassians into battle slaughtered other Christians who had followed the raven banner of Sigurd in hopes of plunder, and no one was thinking of God at all.

The end of the day witnessed a total victory for the Irish.

No little birds sang their sleepy twilight songs in the splintered and trampled pockets of woodland that dotted the battleground. Birdsong could not compete with the pitiful cries of the dying.

When the first shouts of triumph reached the Árd Rí in his tent, he knew his army had won. It was over, then. Everything was over. Brian dismissed his bodyguards to join the celebration. They did not want to leave him, but he insisted. He needed to be left alone with his thoughts.

Accompanied only by his faithful servant, Brian Boru knelt and bowed his head over his folded hands.

* * * * * * * * *

CHAPTER FOURTEEN

SUNSET

His deeply lined face was gaunt with fatigue. The alchemy of time had turned the Celtic copper of his hair to silver. He might have been any old man at his prayers, except for the sudden fire in Brian's eyes when Brodir burst into his tent, and the speed with which he reached for his sword.

The dark and desperate Dane could not make sense of the world around him. As far as he could see in the dusk the earth was littered with dismembered bodies and broken weapons; already the ravens were dropping out of the sky to feed. The battle should have been won long ago. Long ago ... in the morning ... he could remember the morning clearly enough, when the great fleet unloaded enough men to overrun Ireland. Or so it had seemed then. The battle began with a clash and a curse and victory had seemed certain. Then.

The Irish had fought back but that was to be expected. What Brodir and the other leaders had not expected was the sheer stubborn determination of the Gael. It seemed as if every one of them fought like ten. Blood must be shed for every foot of ground gained. Hundreds of warriors on both sides fell in the initial charge, and then more. And more. Died screaming. The battle had swirled over the land like a storm at sea, unpredictable and uncontrollable. Brodir had killed his share several times over but still they came at him. His axe sang its grisly song again and again and still they came at him.

Eventually the Irish were driven as far as an oak forest, Brodir recalled that clearly enough. Too clearly. Among the ancient trees he had seen deeds done that even he would rather forget. He had been a Christian once ...

No victory could be assured in so dense a forest, and in time the survivors had battled their way out into the light again. That was when things became very confused in Brodir's mind. Was it possible his Vikings had retreated? He could not be certain. The fighting continued on and on and then there was the water ...

Blood-red water.

Brodir had made his living on the water but he did

not intend to die on it. He gave up any idea of fighting and fled, clutching his gory axe to his breast as a mother might clutch her child. He wanted to make it into the sanctuary of the trees again, wherever they were ...

Two of his men followed him through the haunted night. They would have followed anyone at that stage; their own senses had left them. As they stumbled over the dead and dying they heard the first shouts of victory. Not the voices of the Valkyries coming to claim their heroes, but the triumphant cries of the Irish.

Up ahead Brodir could see a small glow of light. He ran towards it like a moth to a flame with his companions right behind him.

According to the chronicles, Laiten told Brian, 'There are some people coming towards us.'

The high king asked, 'What manner of people?'

'Blue stark-naked people!' cried the boy when he got a good look at them.

In that moment Brian must have known. Vikings in chainmail. There was no time to think any further, no time to assess and plan. Only to act.

As Brodir burst into his tent Brian reached for his sword.

There are several versions of what happened next. Even among the Irish historians there is dispute as to the events of that evening, while the Norse sagas tell a different story altogether.

Some writers depict Brian Boru as a frail old man waiting meekly on his prayer stool while Brodir struck him down. This seems unlikely to those who have made a study of his character based on his known actions. Throughout his long life Brian was a vigorous, robust individual, a battle-hardened warrior who had fought in combat only the year before and had remained strong enough to ride a horse halfway across Ireland. His sons had not asked him to step aside because he could not fight, only because they feared he might be killed in battle. Ireland truly could not spare him, as later events would show.

Brian had his mighty sword with him. It was a powerful symbol of his warrior status and he never went anywhere without it, certainly not onto a battlefield. The weapon was as much a part of him as his right arm. Nor did he cease to be Brian Boru because he had ceased to lead the army. He may have been old and weary, but the imperative of survival was an automatic reflex with him. It is reasonable to assume that Brian fought for his life.

According to *Cogadh Gaedhel re Gallaibh:* 'Brodir ... was carrying his trusty battle axe, with the handle set in the middle of it. When Brian saw him he gazed at him, and gave him a stroke with his sword and cut off his left leg at the knee and his right leg at the foot. The foreigner dealt Brian a stroke which cleft his head utterly; and Brian killed the second man that was with Brodir, and they fell mutually by each other.'

P W Joyce in his *History of Gaelic Ireland* tells much the same story, without the reference to the second Viking. He adds, 'Brian's guards, as if struck by a sudden sense of danger, returned in haste; but too late.'

In *Cashel of the Kings,* John Gleeson maintains that with a swing of his sword Brian cut off Brodir's left leg below the knee and the right above the ankle. If this is so, the power remaining in the old warrior's shoulders must have been mighty indeed. Brodir was as good as dead even before his axe smashed into Brian's skull.

Brian Boru, King of Ireland, disagrees. Roger Chatterton Newman writes, 'It is unlikely that a man of seventy-three, weary and mourning the loss of one or more sons, would have found the strength to protect himself against sudden assault.' Newman believes the Viking axe fell on an undefended head.

The story as told by the Scandinavians reflects their point of view and is very revealing. *Njal's Saga* relates that Brodir 'rushed from the woods, broke through the entire shield-castle and levelled a blow at the king. The lad Tadk [Laiten] raised his arm to ward off the blow, but the stroke cut off his arm and the king's head. The king's blood ran upon the arm stump and the wound healed immediately.'

The saga goes on to state that the Irish surrounded Brodir and his men and took them alive. They then 'slit open his belly, led him round and round an oak tree, and in this way unwound all of the intestines out of his body, and Brodir did not die before they were all pulled out of him.'

This gruesome detail describes a form of mutilation which was common amongst the Vikings, but never practised by the Irish. The fact that the saga describes Brian's blood as healing an amputated arm shows what high regard the Scandinavians had for Brian Boru himself.

Whatever happened in his tent, the Árd Rí of Ireland was dead. One of the last, and surely the most tragic, fatalities of that fatal day.

The setting sun shed a baleful light over a scene of carnage. The battlefield was hideous to contemplate, littered with the dead and the dying, the dismembered and the maimed.

The terrible rollcall of Irish casualties begins with Brian Boru, his sons Murrough, Flann and Conor, and his grandson Turlough. The swords and axes had done such dreadful work on Good Friday that many other bodies would never be identified. The Irish princes who were recognisable included Mulroney Ua Heyne (Hynes) of Galway and Tadhg Mor Ua Ceallaigh (Kelly), two of the foremost chieftains of Connacht. Also dead was the *tanist* of the Iceadh (Hickey) tribe, who were Dalcassians and the hereditary physicians to the kings of Thomond; Scannlan Ua Cearbhaill (Carroll) lord of Offaly; Dubhagan (Duggan), descended from the druid Mogh Roth; Mac Beatha, lord of Ciarraigh (Kerry); Ua Domhnall (Donnell) lord of Corca Bhaiscinn; at least one king of Brefni; Mothla Ua Faelan (Phelan), lord of the Deisi; Maguidhir (Maguire), prince of Fermanagh; and Brian's nephew Conaing. It has been estimated that as many as sixteen hundred members of the Gaelic nobility died that day. Among the thousands without a title were Niall Ua Cuinn (Quinn), Brian's personal bodyguard, plus all three of the Árd Rí's aides-de-camp, and the son of Ospak of Orkney.

Some of the slain Irish princes eventually would be returned to their tribes. The bodies were carried home if possible, but if those were too hideously damaged, at least the heads went home for burial. In keeping with Gaelic tradition the heroes' heads would be tenderly cleaned and presented to their people with appropriate ceremony. That much of ancient Ireland was still alive in 1014.

A number – though probably not all, for there were too many – of the unclaimed corpses were buried by the survivors. Trying to reunite the numerous body parts with their original owners must have been an impossible task. Irish and foreigners went together into unmarked graves. As recently as the late nineteenth century there were still low mounds of earth in the area, described by the locals as burial mounds from the great battle. It was left to the ravens to dispose of whatever remained. The raven goddess called the Morrigan was the ancient goddess of war.

The annalists relate that the Irish wounded were carried back to Kilmainham. Many of them died and were buried there. The site of the encampment, which later came to be known as 'Bully's Acre', is near the Museum of Modern Art. It was the oldest burial ground in Dublin, and still contains a tenth-century granite shaft that once was topped with a cross. On the front of the shaft is the crudely carved image of a short sword.

On Easter Sunday, Brian's son, Donough, arrived from the south, driving a herd of cattle intended to feed the army. Cian, one of the very few survivors of noble rank, told him what had happened to his father and brothers and a large percentage of his fellow Dalcassians. It was too much for a fifteen-year-old to take in. The shock may have had a lasting influence on him. A boy who had been raised as a young Gaelic prince, no doubt praised and petted by all around him, discovered in one horrific day the cruelty of the world in which he lived. Within a very short time Donough became a bitter man out to get whatever he could.

Donough was now the senior member of his clan at the site of the battle. He could no longer simply play at being a warrior. Overnight, a brash boy had to become a man. Perhaps he went to see the battleground for himself, or made an effort to confer with the other survivors. Perhaps he just wandered off by himself and stared out at the sea for a time. At the end of the day a heavy cloak of responsibility had descended on the unprepared shoulders of Brian's youngest son. Whether he was able for it or not, only time would tell.

The foreign leaders who fought in the Battle of Clontarf were slain as surely as the Irish. Some simply disappeared from history, never to surface again. There are few details as to what happened to the survivors of the invasion force. Presumably a small number made it onto the ships and limped home. In *Njal's Saga,* a nobleman in the Hebrides claimed that a warrior had appeared to him in a dream. The bloodspattered stranger said he had come from Ireland. He further related, 'I died where brave men battled; brands did sing in Erin. Many a mace did shatter mail coats, helms were splintered. Sword fight keen I saw there; Sigurd fell in combat. Blood billowed from death wounds. Brian fell, yet he conquered.'

A week later an exhausted Hrafn the Red arrived in the court of Sigurd the Stout. He brought the actual news from Ireland, beginning with the earl's death. After digesting this dismaying information, Sigurd's trusted retainer Flosi asked, 'What else can you tell me of our men?'

Hrafn's reply was typically succinct. 'They were all slain there.'

With admirable restraint compared to the flamboyant hyperbole of other chroniclers, *The Annals of Inisfallen* relates, 'There were also slain in that battle Maelmora, son of Murchad the king of Laigin, together with the princes of the Laigin round him, and the foreigners of the western world were slaughtered in the same battle.' Maelmora himself was killed by Conaing of Desmond, one of the princes who had followed the banner of Brian's son-in-law.

It would appear that the turning point of the battle had come when the Irish left Magh Dumha and headed towards the Valley of the Tolka. Until then, through all the mad confusion, they had given the impression of an army in retreat.

Fifty-two years later William, the bastard duke of Normandy, would employ a similar ruse at the Battle of Hastings. When his warriors could not break through the shield wall Harold Godwine's men maintained on Senlac Ridge, William dispatched a band of cavalry to gallop away as if in full retreat. Exhilarated by what they perceived as victory, many of the Saxons ran after them. This exposed the main body of their army and Harold, king of England, to the enemy, sealing his doom. William the Bastard became William the Conqueror that day.

By pursuing the main body of the apparently retreating Irish towards Magh Dumha the invaders had sealed their doom. The major part of the fighting had been contained in the area which included Tomar's Wood just long enough for the tide to turn – the irresistible spring tide at full flood.

* * * * * * * *

CHAPTER FIFTEEN

AFTERWORD

The dynasty of Brian Boru was almost extinguished at Clontarf. Brian's unrealised plans and dreams died with his severed head – and with his son and heir Murrough, who shared them and was meant to fulfil them.

Brian Boru had not united Ireland. What he had done was to unite a number of quarrelsome Irish tribes, a great accomplishment in so divided a culture. He also had united the foreign settlers with the natives, which would prove to be a more lasting achievement. Following the Battle of Clontarf, conflict gradually ceased between Viking and Gael. They became the Irish together and began to form the Ireland we know today. Had Brian's dynasty remained intact and his descendants inherited his intelligence and strength of character, some of his other plans might have come to fruition. Or perhaps not. We shall never know.

At least the great battle put a stop to the attempted conquest of Ireland. She would retain her sovereignty unchallenged until the coming of the Normans.

Later historians would argue about the actual number of casualties on that April day in 1014, but the best estimates place it at over ten thousand. The leaders on both sides had been slain. Their armies were virtually destroyed. The loss of so many men of fighting age would make an appreciable difference to the Irish as well as to the Scandinavians. Thereafter the Vikings would concentrate their efforts on the larger island to the east, and change British history.

Not everyone in Ireland knew what had occurred at Clontarf. Years later the Battle of Glenmama was still being described as 'the great battle'. Clontarf had been too overwhelming; it would take a long time for knowledge of the event and its ramifications to trickle down to the populace at large. Outside the sphere of tribal politics ordinary men and women went about their lives free from the insistent clamour of modern communications. Many lived their entire lives without knowing what happened thirty miles away. Several generations would pass before every child in Ireland was familiar with the name of Brian Boru.

During his lifetime Brian was not universally loved. There were chieftains of the Gael who would not be sorry to learn that he was dead, sensing that in the vacuum left behind there might be some advantage to themselves. But first he must be buried; he was the Árd Rí, and recognised as exceptional even by his enemies.

When they learned of Brian's death, monks from the monastery of Sord-Colum-cille, modern-day Swords, rushed to the battlefield to collect his body. According to tradition, a warrior king was carried from the battle-field on the shields of his men. On the way to Swords, Brian may have been surrounded by the heads of his slain captains, serving as a grisly honour guard. If so, this is a harkening back to pagan times that would not have been approved by the clergy. The claim that Brian's sword was laid on his body and a crucifix placed in his hands has not been disputed. His life had been a balancing act between these two symbols.

The monks carried the body of the slain high king to the religious house of St Kieran to be washed and prepared for burial. Meanwhile, messengers were dispatched to Armagh. Archbishop Marianus immediately hurried southward with members of his clergy to supervise the carrying of Brian's body to St Patrick's Cathedral at Armagh. There, amidst splendid trappings and unparalleled demonstrations of public mourning, Brian Boru was waked for twelve days and twelve nights, the longest wake in Irish history. The tradition of the wake recalls the ancient belief that the spirit lingers near the body for several days after death.

For this occasion the various princes of the Uí Néill put aside whatever reservations they had about the Dalcassian usurper and joined in what seems to have been a genuine outpouring of grief.

After his wake the Árd Rí was laid to rest in solitary splendour in a new tomb of hewn marble at the north side of the cathedral, the traditional side for heroes fallen in battle. It is generally believed that his son Murrough was placed in a separate tomb nearby, but there is another intriguing possibility. On the last night of his life Murrough supposedly told his comrades that he would like to rest at Kilmainham when the battle was over. Could the granite shaft in Bully's Acre with its crudely carved sword mark the final resting place of Brian Boru's oldest son?

The Armagh Cathedral of today is a late nineteenth-century reconstruction which replaced a thirteenth-century structure on the site of a still older timber building that was destroyed by fire in 1020. Presumably this last was where Brian was entombed. The exact location of his tomb has long since been lost.

After allowing the tattered remnants of the Irish army several days' rest on Fair Green, young Donough claimed command and they began the long march home, carrying their wounded on litters. During this march they were attacked by Mac Gilla Patrick, prince of Ossory, who was an old enemy of the Dalcassians. Donough ordered the ill and injured to stand aside from the battle, but their fighting spirit remained intact. They insisted on cutting stakes from the forest and tying themselves to them so they could face the enemy on their feet. Observing this, the men of Ossory supposedly were shamed and refused to fight them. It was left to Mac Gilla Patrick himself to follow the survivors of Clontarf and harry them from behind.

It was a bad omen. With Brian Boru gone, the unity he had tried so hard to encourage started to disintegrate. The tribes of Thomond and Desmond went their separate ways. The Owenachts and the Dalcassians began to quarrel over the kingship of Munster.

Malachy Mór, whose adherents insisted he was the real hero of Clontarf – Malachy himself modestly made no such claim – succeeded Brian Boru as high king. There was no one else of sufficient stature and the title was given to him by common consent, although without formality. Once again, Malachy did his best. But he was getting old himself, and his second term of office was no more memorable than his first. There were no real achievements: frenetic little battles for his warriors, sumptuous banquets for his friends.

Malachy reigned as Árd Rí for eight more years, after which he retired to an island in Lough Ennel to spend his last days in prayer and contemplation. When he died – like Brian, in his seventy-third year – the annals celebrated Malachy Mór as 'the pillar of the dignity and nobility of the west of the world'.

By this time the Norse who had settled in Ireland had become the Hiberno-Norse, having adopted not only the customs of their neighbours but also their language. As for the Danes, an old Irish manuscript states that after Clontarf, 'no Danes were left in Ireland except for such a number of merchants and artisans in the cities as could be easily mastered if they dared to rebel.' In the years to come there were very few new arrivals, and none interested in making Ireland a Scandinavian kingdom.

After Malachy Mór's death Ireland had no universally recognised over-king. The affairs of the kingdom were administered for a brief time by a poet-historian called Cian Ua Lochlan and a cleric from Lismore, known as

Corcoran. Their exact functions are unknown, but the Annals of Clonmacnois claim that during their tenure 'the land was governed like a free state and not like a monarchy'.

This soon gave way to a confused period during which kings from both Munster and Connacht competed to become the Árd Rí. Known as 'kings in opposition' rather than high kings, they lacked sufficient support outside of their own tribes. They became little more than a footnote in Irish history, another pitiful example of divisiveness.

The first of these was Brian Boru's youngest son, Donough. When his half-brother Tadhg followed in the family tradition by being elected as king of Munster, Donough set out to plunder neighbouring kingdoms as the first step towards winning the high kingship for himself. He forced Leinster, Ossory and Meath to give him hostages as tokens of their submission, but his hollow claim to be Árd Rí was never fully accepted.

Tadhg also was finding kingship difficult to maintain. In 1019 there was a revolt against him in Clare in which which Donough lost his right hand. In 1023 Tadhg was killed, ostensibly by one of the rebellious tribes, although many believed Donough was the instigator. He may not have inherited the noble qualities of his late father, but

Donough certainly had his share of ambition.

When Tadhg was dead, Donough claimed the kingship of Munster. He lacked the military strength to hold it. For the sake of his father the Dalcassians supported him, but they would have to wait for another generation of warriors to mature after the massive losses at Clontarf before they could field a substantial army. Taking full advantage of their weakness, the Owenachts seized Cashel.

The Irish victory at Clontarf had been a mixed blessing. In the short term it had prevented a foreign conquest, but in the long term the loss of Brian Boru was a disaster. The subsequent reversion to tribalism and the resulting lack of a cohesive overall policy of defence left Ireland vulnerable to invasion.

Malachy Mór had been the last true Árd Rí. After him the title would cease to have any meaning. There would be a total of six 'kings in opposition'. The bad-tempered struggle between Gaelic princes seeking supreme power would continue until the death of Ruaidri O'Connor of Connacht in 1198.

Although he had not shown himself as a hero during the Battle of Clontarf, Sitric Silkbeard continued to rule as king of Dublin. The royal household included both his wife, Emer, who was Brian Boru's daughter, and Sitric's mother, Gormlaith, whose undying hatred for Brian must have kept the home fires blazing. Perhaps it was Sitric's punishment for his sins to be caught between these two women.

Like the Vikings, Sitric Silkbeard was not all bad. He was instrumental in gaining Dublin a reputation abroad as a major trading centre, even though it was not the political centre of Ireland. Under his influence the city became Christianised. Several years after Gormlaith died, Sitric built a church in 1030 which he dedicated to St Olaf, perhaps in honour of his father, Olaf Cuaran, or one of his own sons by the same name who was killed by the Saxons while on a pilgrimage to Rome. St Olaf's eventually was replaced by Christchurch Cathedral, which still stands today. It is very close to the site of the ancient Viking palace. Sitric died in 1042 on another pilgrimage to Rome, but is best known by historians for introducing coinage into Ireland.

Of all those who fought and died on that Good Friday in Ireland, only Brian Boru would be honoured by subsequent generations as a great hero. Mythology aside, from his actions it is apparent that he was as different from most men of his time as were Caesar or Charlemagne from the men of theirs. Brian must have possessed great determination and a powerful ego to sustain him through his long life. After his wild youth he grew into a thoughtful, mature individual who tried whenever possible to behave with honour. No one knows just what dreams Brian dreamed for Ireland. But he was a man who made careful plans. And he was well aware of the larger world.

Had Brian and his sons survived the Battle of Clontarf the subsequent history of Ireland might have been very different. When the time came, Murrough would have made a formidable high king. He had the necessary gifts: courage and education and a strong tribe behind him. In addition, he was a proven leader who inspired others. It is likely that his younger brothers would have supported him rather than seeking the title for themselves. They appear to have been a close family ... until the shock of Clontarf.

Thanks to Brian's efforts, Murrough was well prepared to continue the work his father had begun. Based on what Brian already had achieved it is not unreasonable to assume that this would include the establishment of a centralised form of governance, as well as a strong standing army to protect the country from future invaders. The freedom and sovereignty of Ireland might have been secured for centuries to come.

Sadly, the next wave of invaders encountered neither a standing army nor a unified people. Tribal warfare was once more endemic. The Normans, led by Strongbow, opened the gate to Ireland in 1170. Within a few years the English marched in.

KINCORA

Oh, where, Kincora! is Brian the Great?
And where is the beauty that once was thine?
Oh, where are the princes and nobles that sate
At the feast in thy halls, and drank the red wine?
      Where, oh, Kincora?

Oh, where, Kincora! are thy valorous lords?
Oh, whither, thou Hospitable, are they gone?
Oh, where are the Dalcassians of the Golden Swords?
And where are the warriors Brian led on?
      Where, oh, Kincora?

And where is Murrough, the descendant of kings –
The defeater of a hundred – the daringly brave –
Who set but slight store by jewels and rings –
Who swam down the torrent and laughed at its wave?
  Where, oh, Kincora?

And where is Donough, King Brian's worthy son?
And where is Conaing, the Beautiful Chief?
And Kian, and Corc, alas! They are gone –
They have left me this night alone with my grief.
  Left me, Kincora!

And where are the chiefs with whom Brian went forth,
The ne'er vanquished sons of Erin the Brave,
The great king of Onacht, renowned for his worth,
And the hosts of Baskinn, from the western wave?
  Where, oh, Kincora?

Oh, where is Duvlann of the swift-footed Steeds?
And where is Cian, who was son of Molloy?
And where is King Lonergan, the fame of whose deeds
In the red battlefield no time can destroy?
  Where, oh, Kincora?

And where is that youth of majestic height,
The faith keeping Prince of the Scots? – Even he,
As wide as his fame was, as great as his might,
Was tributary, oh, Kincora, to thee!
    Thee, oh, Kincora!

They are gone, those heroes of royal birth,
Who plundered no churches, and broke no trust,
'Tis weary for me to be living on earth
While they, oh, Kincora, lie low in the dust!
    Low, oh, Kincora!

Oh, never again will princes appear
To rival the Dalcassians of Cleaving Swords!
I can never dream of meeting, afar or anear,
In the east or the west, such heroes and lords!
    Never, Kincora!

Dear are the images my memory calls up
Of Brian Boru! – how he would never miss
To give me at the banquet the first bright cup!
Oh, why did he heap on me honour like this?
    Why, oh, Kincora?

I am Mac Liag, and my home is on the lake;
Thither often, to that place whose beauty has fled,
Came Brian to ask me, and I went for his sake,
Oh, my grief! that I should live, and Brian be dead!
    Dead, oh, Kincora?

Attributed to Mac Liag (c. 1015)

Translated from the Irish by James Clarence Mangan (1803-1849)

SELECT BIBLIOGRAPHY

Almgren, Bertil, Prof., chief contributor, THE VIKING. Crescent Books, New York, by arrangement with AB Nordbok, Gothenburg, Sweden: 1975

Bardon, Jonathan, and Conlin, Stephen, DUBLIN; ONE THOUSAND YEARS OF WOOD QUAY. The Blackstaff Press, Belfast: 1984

Bartlett, Thomas, and Jeffery, Keith, A MILITARY HISTORY OF IRELAND. Cambridge University Press, Cambridge: 1996

Bayerschmidt, Carl, and Hollander, Lee, translators, NJÁL'S SAGA. Twayne Publishers, New York, and the American–Scandinavian Foundation, New York: 1955

Bradley, John, editor, VIKING DUBLIN EXPOSED. The O'Brien Press, Dublin: 1984

Bugge, Alexander, translator, *CAITHREIM CELLACHAIN CAISIL* (Callahan of Cashel). Christiana Press, Norway: 1905

Byrne, Francis John, IRISH KINGS AND HIGH KINGS. St. Martin's Press, New York: 1973

Chatterton, E. Keble, SAILING SHIPS AND THEIR STORY. Argosy-Antiquarian Ltd., New York: 1968

Clarke, Howard B., DUBLIN C. 840 – C. 1540. The Friends of Medieval Dublin and The Ordnance Survey, Dublin: 1978

Cook, Jean, HISTORY'S TIMELINE. Crescent Books, New York: 1981

Curtis, Edmund, A HISTORY OF IRELAND. Methuen, London: 1952

Delaney, Frank, THE CELTS. Hodder & Stoughton, London: 1986

Dillon, Myles, THE CYCLES OF THE KINGS. Oxford University Press, London: 1946

Dillon, Myles, THE TABOOS OF THE KINGS OF IRELAND. The Royal Irish Academy, Dublin: 1951

Duffy, Seán, editor, THE MACMILLAN ATLAS OF IRISH HISTORY. Macmillan, New York: 1997

Dunlevy, Mairéad, DRESS IN IRELAND, B. T. Batsford Ltd, London: 1989

Ferguson, Lady, THE STORY OF THE IRISH BEFORE THE CONQUEST. Sealy, Bryers and Walker, Dublin: 1903

Flood, J. M., THE NORTHMEN IN IRELAND. Browne and Nolan Ltd., London: no date

Frost, James, THE HISTORY AND TOPOGRAPHY OF THE COUNTY OF CLARE. Mercier Press, Dublin: 1978

Fry, Peter, and Somerset, Fiona, THE HISTORY OF SCOTLAND. Barnes & Noble, New York: 1995

Gibbs-Smith, Charles H., THE BAYEUX TAPESTRY. Phaidon Press Ltd, London: 1973

Ginnell, Laurence, THE BREHON LAWS. T. Fisher Unwin, London: 1894

Gleeson, Rev. John, CASHEL OF THE KINGS. DeBurca Rare Books, Dublin: 2001

Gwynn, John, editor, THE BOOK OF ARMAGH. Royal Irish Academy, Dublin: 1913.

Hayes-McCoy, G. A., IRISH BATTLES. Gill and Macmillan, Dublin: 1980

Hime, M C., BRIAN BORU AND THE BATTLE OF CLONTARF. Sullivan Brothers, Dublin: 1889

Hull, Eleanor, A HISTORY OF IRELAND, VOL. ONE. Phoenix Publishing Co. Dublin: no date

Jones, Gwyn, A HISTORY OF THE VIKINGS, Oxford University Press, London: 1968

Joyce, Patrick Weston, SOCIAL HISTORY OF ANCIENT IRELAND, VOLS. ONE and TWO. Benjamin Blom, New York: 1913; reprinted by Arno Press, New York: 1980

Kelly, Fergus, A GUIDE TO EARLY IRISH LAW. Dublin Institute for Advanced Studies, Dublin: 1988

Kierse, Seán, HISTORIC KILLALOE. Boru Books, Killaloe: 1983

Lincoln, Colm, DUBLIN AS A WORK OF ART. The O'Brien Press, Dublin: 1992

Little, Dr. George A., DUBLIN BEFORE THE VIKINGS. M. H. Gill & Son Ltd., Dublin: 1957

Mac Airt, Seán, editor and translator, ANNALS OF INISFALLEN. Dublin Institute for Advanced Studies, Dublin: 1951

Mackie, J. D., A HISTORY OF SCOTLAND. Dorset Press, New York: 1978

MacManus, Seán, BRIAN'S BATTLE AS IT IS TOLD IN THE NORSE SAGA. Three Candles, Dublin: 1933

McCullough, David Willis, WARS OF THE IRISH KINGS. History Book Club, New York: 2000

McIntyre, Dennis, THE MEADOW OF THE BULL, A History of Clontarf. Future Print Ltd., Dublin: 1987

McWhiney, Grady, and Jamieson, Perry D., ATTACK AND DIE. University of Alabama Press, Alabama: 1982

Mitchell, Frank, SHELL GUIDE TO READING THE IRISH LANDSCAPE. Country House, Dublin: 1987

Murphy, Rev. Denis, editor, THE ANNALS OF CLONMACNOISE. Dublin University Press, Dublin: 1896

Newman, Roger Chatterton, BRIAN BORU, King of Ireland. Anvil Books, Dublin: 1983

O'Brien, Donough, HISTORY OF THE O'BRIENS. B. T. Batsford, Ltd., New York: 1949

Ó Corráin, Donncha, IRELAND BEFORE THE NORMANS. Gill and Macmillan, Dublin: 1972

O'Donnell, E. E., THE ANNALS OF DUBLIN. Wolfhound Press, Dublin: 1987

O'Donoghue, John, HISTORICAL MEMOIR OF THE O'BRIENS. Hodges, Smith & Co., Dublin: 1860

O'Donovan, John, translator, ANNALS OF THE KINGDOM OF IRELAND by the Four Masters, VOL. TWO. Hodges, Smith & Co., Dublin: 1856; third edition by de Burca Rare Books, Dublin: 1990.

O'Donovan, John, translator, THE BOOK OF RIGHTS. Printed for the Celtic Society, Dublin: 1847

Oliver, Neil, VIKINGS, A HISTORY. Weidenfeld & Nicolson, London, by arrangement with the British Broadcasting Co.: 2012

Richter, Michael, MEDIEVAL IRELAND. Gill & Macmillan, Dublin: 1988

Ryan, Etienne, editor, NORTH MUNSTER STUDIES. Thomond Archaeological Society, Limerick: 1967

Ryan, Rev. John, THE BATTLE OF CLONTARF. The Journal of the Royal Society of Antiquaries of Ireland, Dublin: 1938

Shetelig, Haakon, VIKING HISTORY OF WESTERN EUROPE. University of Oslo, Sweden: 1940

Slavin, Michael, THE ANCIENT BOOKS OF IRELAND. Wolfhound Press, Dublin: 2005

Smyth, Alfred P., CELTIC LEINSTER. The Irish Academic Press, Dublin: 1982

Smyth, Alfred P., SCANDINAVIAN YORK AND DUBLIN, The Irish Academic Press, Dublin: 1987

Stenton, Sir Frank, ANGLO-SAXON ENGLAND. Oxford University Press, London: 1970

Sturlason, Snorre, HEIMSKRINGLA, or the Lives of the Norse Kings. Translation by Erling Monsen, Cambridge University Press, London: 1931

Sullivan Brothers, The, THE IRISH CLANS; THEIR BATTLES, CHIEFS, AND PRINCES. Dublin: no date

Todd, James Henthorn, *COGADH GAEDHEL RE GALLAIBH, the* WAR OF THE IRISH WITH THE FOREIGNERS, from the Original Irish Text, with Translation and Introduction. Longmans, Green, Reader and Dyer, London: 1867

Ua Clerigh, Arthur, THE HISTORY OF IRELAND TO THE COMING OF HENRY II. T. Fisher Unwin, Dublin: no date

Weir, Hugh, BRIAN BORU, Ballinaskella Press, Clare: 2002

White, the Very Rev. Patrick, HISTORY OF CLARE AND THE DALCASSIAN CLANS. M. H. Gill & Son, Dublin: 1893

Worsaae, Jens; Henry, David, editor, VIKING IRELAND. Pinkfoot Press, Belgavies, Scotland: 1995